THE B___ST. LOUIS SPORTS ARGUMENTS

THE 100 MOST CONTROVERSIAL, DEBATABLE QUESTIONS FOR DIE-HARD FANS

BRYAN BURWELL

SOURCEBOOKS, INC.
NAPERVILLE, ILLINOIS

Published by Sourcebooks, Inc.
P.O. Box 4410, Naperville, Illinois 60567-4410
(630) 961-3900
Fax: (630) 961-2168
www.sourcebooks.com

Library of Congress Cataloging-in-Publication Data

Burwell, Bryan.
  The best St. Louis sports arguments : the 100 most controversial, debatable questions for die-hard St. Louis fans / Bryan Burwell.
     p. cm.
  Includes index.
  ISBN-13: 978-1-4022-1104-1 (pbk.)
  ISBN-10: 1-4022-1104-X (pbk.)
  1. Sports—Missouri—Saint Louis—History. 2. Saint Louis (Mo.)—Social life and customs. I. Title.

GV584.5.S787 2007
796'.0977866—dc22

                                            2007031069

Printed and bound in the United States of America.
       CH 10 9 8 7 6 5 4 3 2 1

Also by Bryan Burwell

At the Buzzer! Havlicek Steals, Erving Soars, Magic Deals,
Michael Scores:
The Greatest Moments in NBA History

To Dawnn and Victoria: Thanks for your patience with all my weird writer's hours and sleepless nights; thanks most of all for the kindness and for all the meals you served me in "the dungeon."

CONTENTS

THE BEST ST. LOUIS SPORTS ARGUMENTS

THE TEAM'S THE THING: THE BEST PRO TEAMS IN
ST. LOUIS HISTORY

HOW SWEET (AND AWFUL) IT IS: THE BEST (AND WORST)
TRADES IN ST. LOUIS HISTORY

TALKIN' BASEBALL

FOOTBALL FEVER

THE BEST ST. LOUIS SPORTS ARGUMENTS

INTRODUCTION

Once you peel away the superficial layers from the sports we love, inevitably we come to these irrefutable truths:

Everyone loves to pick sides.

We are always right and you are always wrong.

The nature of sports—at least from a fan's perspective—is to search for unconditional terms of resolution. We need winners and losers, villains and victims; we must form hard and fast opinions on what we've witnessed, even if the truth is never that rigid. Sometimes it is dicey and complex. Sometimes it is a riddle wrapped in a mystery, tied together nicely by an undeniable conundrum.

Question: Who is the greatest athlete of all time?

Answer: Hmmmm, is it Michael Jordan? Jim Brown? Jim Thorpe?

Now we're on to something: a great sports argument. This book presents 100 of the greatest, most controversial, and highly debatable arguments in St. Louis sports history. If you are a member of that passionate tribe known as the St. Louis Sports Nation, you will find plenty of opportunities to express your opinions as you browse through the following pages. You will choose sides. You might grumble or groan. If we know you like we think we do, you'll probably shake your fist, curl your lip, or perhaps occasionally even nod agreeably. You are a St. Louis sports fan, so we're about to give you something to shout about.

Do you remember the night when that bleepin' Don Denkinger ruined my life??!!!

Well, what if I told you it wasn't Denkinger's fault that the Cards lost the 1985 World Series? Would that get you started? Would that run your blood pressure up to a boil, or just a controlled simmer?

Who is most responsible for the Rams losing Super Bowl XXXVI, Mike Martz or Bill Belichick?

Now that conversation ought to stir a little emotion. Over the past few months, I have leaned on some of my best friends—long-time St. Louis sports wise guys, all of them legendary press box trash talkers and radio, TV, and print debaters—for their thoughts. Many thanks go to Mike Claiborne, Frank Cusumano, Rick ("The Commish") Hummel, Jim Thomas, Jim ("The Cat") Hayes, Greg Marecek, Joe Buck, Martin Kilcoyne, Maurice Drummond, Chris (Blogger Boy) Pelican, Bernie Miklasz, Vahe Gregorian, Tim McKernan, Joe Strauss, Derrick Goold, Steve Korte, Bill Coats, Howard Balzer, and Randy Karraker, plus legendary former coach Jim Hanifan and noted author Jonathan Eig. Even when they didn't realize it, the little verbal sparring sessions we had on game days, in pressrooms, or in studio bullpens provided invaluable research for this project. They helped show me that sometimes there is no right or wrong answer in sports, only an opinion. Trust me, with these guys, there were always plenty of opinions.

As you read through these pages, let yourself go. Stomp your feet and scream to the heavens. Be totally convinced that you are right and we are wrong. That's part of the irrefutable truth of sports. Feel free to cuss us out or cajole us.

It's sports.

It's supposed to be fun.

It's supposed to be debatable.

It's supposed to raise your blood pressure and a few hairs on the back of your neck.

Bryan Burwell
Wildwood, Missouri

TOP OF THE TOWN

WHO WERE THE MOST NOTABLE FIGURES IN ST. LOUIS SPORTS HISTORY?

Of all the colorful questions and competitive arguments that I encountered while trying to sort through facts and dissect opinions on the most highly debatable and ultimately controversial arguments in St. Louis sports, none generated more pause for reflection and brain-twisting anxiety than this little pearl.

Pick the figures in this city's rich and memorable sports history that belong on the imaginary Mount Rushmore of St. Louis sports.

Now consider that question for a moment and mull over the myriad of potential qualities and qualifications that come with it:

Does it mean the most famous?

Does it mean the greatest?

Does it mean the most popular or beloved?

Does it require that you include a mixed bag of athletic diversity (one figure from baseball, one from football, one from hockey, one from soccer, etc....)? Or maybe it means that in a town most notable for its true devotion to baseball, the only way to certify St. Louis as America's ultimate baseball town is to chisel the mountainside with nothing but Cardinals red.

The longer we searched for the simple answers, the more we realized that there are no simple answers, even after endless conversations with some of this town's finest sports authorities. The sentiments and sensibilities of every sports lover in St. Louis seemed certain of only one name (can you guess who that is?), while a second tier of seven others seemed to constantly shift due to different generations and sports passions. Basically, what I discovered is that you have to dispel the conventional wisdom that our town's Mount Rushmore must be limited to only four names.

That was a mission impossible I could not solve. We needed to widen the face of this mountainside and broaden the selection process—there are just too many great names and warm sentiments to consider. So the mountain has been changed to accommodate a more inclusive list of all-time greats. What we have here is our collection of St. Louis' most honored figures across all sports generations. You may not agree with the order, but I doubt anyone will argue that any of these men—and one woman—do not belong among the most notable names in St. Louis sports history.

WHO WERE BASEBALL'S BEST?

1 Since this is St. Louis, it goes without saying that the first argument in this book ought to hinge around baseball. However, generations of baseball legends have played in St. Louis, which makes narrowing down the list of all-time greats even more challenging.

9. JAMES "COOL PAPA" BELL

"So many people say I was born too early, but that's not true—they opened the doors too late."

—James "Cool Papa" Bell

This famous sentence, often uttered whenever anyone started feeling sorry that one of the finest baseball players in history never had a chance to display his gifts in the major leagues, easily sums up the life story of James "Cool Papa" Bell.

James Thomas Bell was born to a sharecropper on May 17, 1903, in Starkville, Mississippi. Seventeen years later he and his family moved to St. Louis, where his baseball career began. Bell was a knuckleball pitcher for a local semi-pro team, Compton Hill. Unfortunately, that was 27 years before major league baseball would integrate and allow black players into the big leagues. But that didn't stop him from becoming one of the best players in baseball history, ultimately developing into a Hall of Fame star in the Negro Leagues.

Within two seasons, the kid was in the Negro National League, signing with the St. Louis Stars for $90 a month. Soon after that, he earned one of the best nicknames in sports. The 19-year-old was facing one of the most feared batters in the Negro Leagues, future Hall of Famer Oscar Charleston, and calmly struck him out. Teammates immediately called him "cool," and Stars' manager Bill Gatewood spiced it up by calling him a "cool papa." Thus, Bell was christened "Cool Papa" Bell.

Luckily for Bell, Gatewood had an eye for talent as well as a gift for clever nicknames. Soon after joining the Stars, Gatewood started playing Bell in the outfield when he was between pitching starts, utilizing the kid's blinding speed to track down every fly ball and generate tons of stolen bases. Within four years, he was a full-time everyday player and the finest leadoff hitter in the Negro Leagues.

"Cool Papa" spent 10 years in St. Louis playing for the Stars, winning Negro League titles in 1929 and 1930, before heading off to play in South America after the original Negro National League folded. He returned to the United States in 1933, joining the newly revamped Negro League. Bell then spent six years with one of the most

5

outstanding teams in the history of baseball, white or black—the Pittsburgh Crawfords.

The Crawfords were studded with future Hall of Famers like Bell, Josh Gibson, Oscar Charleston, Judy Johnson, and Satchel Paige. Unfortunately, no accurate statistics were kept during those early years in the Negro Leagues. However, most baseball historians believe Bell's career batting average was at least .340. In addition, some estimate he may have stolen more than 175 bases in one season.

Bell, who was finally inducted into baseball's Hall of Fame in 1974, spent the rest of his life in St. Louis. By 1947, when Jackie Robinson integrated major league baseball, Bell's career was nearing the end. He retired as a player in 1948, then spent several years managing one of the KC Monarchs' farm teams. Thus, he missed out on the first wave of integration in the major leagues. In 1951, the St. Louis Browns offered Bell a contract, but by then Bell was 48 years old. He turned them down because he knew he could no longer play at a high enough level to compete in the majors.

St. Louis never forgot "Cool Papa," even after he retired and spent more than 20 years working as a custodian and night watchman at city hall. In 1987, Dickson Avenue was renamed James "Cool Papa" Bell Avenue in his honor. Two months after his death on March 7, 1991, "Cool Papa" Bell was given a star on the St. Louis Walk of Fame on Delmar Avenue in the city's famous Loop.

8. MARK McGWIRE

Anyone in St. Louis who's read my columns in the *Post-Dispatch* over the past few years knows exactly how I feel about Mark McGwire. Long before his embarrassing congressional testimony on Capitol Hill that broke the hearts of so many of his devoted fans, I firmly believed Big Mac was a steroid-using cheat whose historic home runs were tainted.

But I also know that the hero-worshipping business is difficult to understand. We prefer to embrace the fantasy and block out the obvious imperfections or ambiguities that might conspire to wreck our giddy dreams. So it's impossible to ignore those 70 home runs he hit in the summer of 1998 and the immediate impact he had on baseball's nationwide revival, spawning a Big Mac lovefest here in Cardinals Nation.

So despite my angst about him, I understand that he must be on our tally of notable St. Louis sports figures; after all, 70 home runs *is* 70 home runs. When a player breaks one of baseball's most relevant single-season records—regardless of how you think he did it—he belongs on this list.

What makes McGwire even more notable is how that stunning accomplishment has half the town feeling he should be famous, and the other half cursing his infamy. No St. Louis sports figure other than McGwire has ever generated that sort of complex love and hate, which is why he must be a significant name on this list. I have come to grips with this, thanks in large part to my good friend and sports

7

radio gadfly Brian McKenna, who put McGwire into his proper context in the lore of St. Louis sports history:

"Every time I think of what happened to St. Louis regarding Big Mac, it feels like a guy who firmly believed that the best day in his life was the day he got married to his beautiful wife," said McKenna. "And then five years later he finds out on that wonderful day his lovely bride just happened to sleep with every guy in the wedding party.

"Uhhh, it sort of changes the hell out of that perfect day, doesn't it?" McKenna asked. "Well that's how a lot of us feel about McGwire. That summer of '98 was the best baseball summer of our lives until we saw Big Mac sitting in front of that congressional hearing saying, 'I'm not here to talk about the past.' He cheated, and now that we know it, it spoils everything."

The perfect example of what McGwire means to most of Cardinals Nation happened on September 30, 2005, when Big Mac returned to old Busch Stadium in its final days and received a mostly warm, but mixed, welcome home. The fans loved him in spite of what he did to them six months earlier in Washington, D.C. They tried to forget about his shrinking legitimacy after that rather awkward testimony before a congressional hearing investigating steroid abuse.

It made a lot of Big Mac fans squirm as he refused to refute the popular notion that his greatest baseball accomplishments were tainted by steroids.

They all wanted to hear him say something different.

But in D.C., and again on his return to Cardinals Nation, Big Mac kept his mouth shut. He didn't deny anything. He didn't tell us one word that would make anyone believe what happened in front of Congress was all some sad mistake.

But that Busch Stadium finale did prove one thing: Most people still love him, but a growing number no longer do.

"I'm not here to talk about the past...." Those are the words McGwire will live with forever. Those words will define his legacy and haunt him until—or if—the Hall of Fame voters no longer snub him. But I wonder how much those words damaged his reputation in St. Louis. You have to know that there are still people in this town who are going to cheer him no matter what. They will cling with blind-faith devotion to McGwire because in their minds he will always be one of Major League Baseball's greatest boys of summer.

To me, he'll always be something a lot less than that.

7. DIZZY DEAN

When you think of old-school Cardinals, Dizzy Dean immediately comes to mind. He falls into the same category as the next fellow on our list, Rogers Hornsby—legends whose most devoted fan base has dwindled because of time.

But for those old enough to remember, the right-handed pitcher was one of the original sports eccentrics and the quintessential member of the rowdy "Gas House Gang" of the 1930s.

9

Inducted into the baseball Hall of Fame in 1953, Dean is the only pitcher in Cardinals history—and the last man in the National League—to win 30 games (1934). In his six seasons in St. Louis, Dean led the league in victories twice (30 in 1934 and 28 in 1935), and led the National League in strikeouts for four consecutive seasons. Dizzy still ranks high on nearly every club career pitching list: he's second in strikeouts; third in winning percentage; sixth in victories, complete games, and shutouts; and ninth in innings pitched.

Dean's celebrity grew after his playing days when he became an entertaining broadcaster and one of baseball's greatest ambassadors.

6. ROGERS HORNSBY

We can't forget the old guys. Just because none of us are old enough to have seen Rogers Hornsby play, there's no way to forget what kind of talent the Cardinals Hall of Fame second baseman was.

Since 1900, only two men have batted .400 three times: Ty Cobb and Hornsby. Hornsby is also one of only two men (Ted Williams is the other) to have won more than one Triple Crown. Those major accomplishments make it easy to place Hornsby this high on the list even though he played in the early 20th century. Hornsby was a great hitter, arguably the best there ever was. During his 23-year career, he posted single-season batting averages of .401,

.403, and a modern-day baseball record of .424 (1924). He led the National League in batting six consecutive seasons (keeping a .397 average during that span). From 1921 through 1925, his batting average soared to .402. No baseball player had ever sustained such excellence over any five-year stretch.

How would you like to pick his greatest season ever?

- 1922: .401 average, 42 homers, 152 RBI, and the Triple Crown
- 1924: .424 average, 25 homers, 94 RBI
- 1925: .403 average, 39 homers, 143 RBI

The 1942 inductee into the Hall of Fame ranks second only to Cobb in career batting average (Cobb is at .366, Hornsby is at .358). The only reason Hornsby is not ranked higher on our list is because few St. Louis sports fans who are alive have the appreciation for him that they have for the other more contemporary heroes.

5. ALBERT PUJOLS

Before his career ends in St. Louis, I can almost guarantee that Albert Pujols will rise much higher on this list of all-time greats in St. Louis sports history. At his current production, it's conceivable that he will end up at the very top, *El Hombre* side by side with Stan "The Man" Musial. (Keep reading for more on "The Man.")

Later in this book, we will continue to document the many reasons why Pujols, in his short time on the St. Louis sports scene, is already considered one of the best to ever play here. Since Pujols has only played six seasons with the Cardinals, I can't justify placing him over the living legend Hall of Famers like Musial, Gibson, Brock, and Smith. But give him time: Pujols is already that good, and he's just getting better.

The numbers are staggering. No one in baseball history has had a better six-year start to a career than Pujols in terms of power, average, run production, and scoring. He is the only player in major league history to hit 30 or more home runs in each of his first six seasons. He was the youngest player to reach 250 home runs (25 years, 258 days), and is on target to become the youngest to reach 300 as well. He's only the fourth player in major league history to have six straight 100 RBI seasons to begin a career. The other three are Hall of Famers Ted Williams, Joe DiMaggio, and Al Simmons.

Talk to Tony La Russa about Pujols and he can't stop gushing. You want to see La Russa smile, just get him talking about Pujols's ability to produce game-winning hits. "Check those stats," La Russa will tell you with a glimmer in his eyes. "Have you checked those stats yet? That's what I love about him the most. It's not how many RBI he has. It's when he has them."

In four of his first six seasons, *El Hombre* has led or shared the major league lead in producing game-winning

RBI. Over that six-year span, he had 121 game-winning RBI and 195 go-ahead RBI.

The Cardinals press guide has eight full pages of biographical and statistical information on Pujols, and it still probably isn't enough to fully capture what he means to the franchise now, because he keeps finding ways to get better.

Pujols possesses one of those things that you love to see in the great ones: the ability to seek out the slightest flaw in a superstar game, then spend every waking moment trying to wipe it out. For example, he is now a Gold Glove first baseman, only a few years after converting from the outfield. He is an outspoken clubhouse leader after coming into the league as a somewhat quiet rookie. After being criticized for being a moody, unapproachable superstar on course to become the next Barry Bonds, Pujols came back in 2007 as a new man in the clubhouse. He is now an approachable, easily quotable star who is unafraid to speak up on important issues affecting his team, the game, and occasionally society.

4. OZZIE SMITH

Style and substance: That is the essence of Ozzie ("The Wizard of Oz") Smith. Off the field, he was always the most impeccable man in the room, with his perfectly matched designer suits, shirts, ties, and shoes. On the field, he was the elegant shortstop with the speed, agility, smarts, and athleticism to get to balls no one else could reach on their best days.

"The Wizard" gobbled them all up on good days and bad, and turned playing shortstop into an art form that could have been set to ballet music. He made the routine entertaining and the spectacular spellbinding. Between 1980 and 1992, he won a remarkable 13 consecutive Gold Gloves and set a major league record with an all-time low of eight errors in 1991.

Every day, he made it fun to watch baseball, gliding across the artificial carpet of Busch, performing his customary acrobatic flips before the game, and providing even more showmanship during the games. Yet as great as he was as a slick-fielding shortstop, Smith's greatest career highlight came courtesy of his bat.

We all remember the moment: Game 5 of the 1985 NL championship. In the bottom of the ninth against the Los Angeles Dodgers, Ozzie came to the plate batting left-handed against reliever Tom Niedenfuer. On a 1–2 pitch, Smith stroked his first left-handed homer in 3,009 career at-bats, prompting the Cardinals' legendary broadcaster Jack Buck to bellow out his most memorable call: "Go crazy, folks! Go crazy!"

3. LOU BROCK

Even though I grew up in Washington, D.C.—an American League city—in the 1960s, I was always captivated by the Cardinals in the National League. One reason was Lou Brock. He was everything I loved about National League baseball back then; he was fast as a whippet on the base paths, graceful in the outfield, and an all-around mixture of power and hitting skill at the plate. Brock's talent altered games. He won eight stolen-base titles, broke the major league record for stolen bases with 118 (in 1974), and topped the century mark for steals at the ripe old age of 35. When he retired, he was the game's greatest base thief, and set the table for St. Louis' fascination with speed in the Whitey Herzog era.

When I finally met him in person, shortly before he retired, as part of an assignment for a national magazine article, I was fascinated by his intelligence as both a student of the base-stealing art form and as a businessman off the field. I remember standing out on the field at old Busch Stadium with him. We talked about base stealing like we were in an advanced college kinesiology class. Brock explained his precise footwork, drilled me on the wasted motion lesser base thieves used, then instructed me on the advantages of a smooth crossover first step in place of a slower, shorter shuffle step.

The passion in his voice let me know that he regarded his craft as equal parts art and science. This was not simply about using the raw speed God blessed him with. It was about using that brain, too. When you were trying to pilfer a base off a rocket arm like Koufax or Marichal, or outrun a cannonball thrown by Roseboro, being fast wasn't going to be enough.

Lou Brock was an artist.

2. BOB GIBSON

What is the measure of a man who redefined the game with his total pitching domination? Bob Gibson was one of the most overpowering, ultra-competitive athletes I've ever seen. In fact, his 1968 season was so magnificent that baseball had to change its rules, lowering the pitcher's mound to level the playing field for hitters. How great was Gibby in 1968? He won 15 consecutive games, had 13 shutouts, struck out 268 batters, and with only 62 walks had a strikeout-to-walk ratio of 5 to 1. But the most memorable aspect of the season was his imposing 1.12 earned run average.

As a kid growing up in D.C., I loved my annual trips to St. Louis, partly because my uncle took me to Cards games in Sportsman's Park and old Busch. I watched Gibson flinging heat and menacing everyone with his delivery, a delivery so hostile toward hitters that it appeared he was about to leg-whip you with that furious follow-through. During the World Series I relished sitting in front of the black and white television watching the Cards with my dad, a St. Louis native. We would cheer for the Redbirds, and I was always fascinated by the sight of Gibby throwing out of the autumn shadows in old Busch. I knew there was something special about him just by the way he carried himself on the field; he was all business and raw intimidation. He was the first athlete I saw who I knew struck fear in an opponent's heart without saying a word, and I quickly began to understand how unique that competitive quality was.

1. STAN MUSIAL

In putting together this list of baseball's best, there was only one name that was universally agreed upon for inclusion: Stan "The Man" Musial. He belongs at the top of any list of St. Louis sports immortals. Although Albert Pujols may one day join Musial as a universally loved and unquestionably respected sports figure, right now Stan "The Man" stands alone as the most significant sports figure in St. Louis history.

Musial's longevity in this market (his entire 22-year career was in St. Louis) surely played a large part in the city's attachment to him. It didn't take long for "The Man" to become "one of us": Musial came in as a rookie in 1942, and in his first full season batted .315. It was the first of 16 consecutive seasons in which he batted over .300.

Why else is he No. 1? He was a member of three World Series championship teams, was selected to play in 24 All-Star Games, was a first-ballot Hall of Famer, and was the first Cardinal to have his uniform number (#6) retired. If Musial had played his entire career in New York instead of St. Louis, he would not have to bother with any of those lists that regard him as one of baseball's most underrated all-time superstars.

But Musial never wanted to leave St. Louis, and that makes him even more appealing to St. Louis fans. They can use him as the ultimate justification that there really is an East Coast–biased sports media that has it in for everything about St. Louis.

Several gifted Hall of Fame baseball players have their bronzed statues outside of Busch Stadium, but one statue stands alone, larger than life, at the ballpark's main gate: the statue of Musial. There's a reason for that, because Stan "The Man" has always been the larger-than-life symbol of Cardinals Nation.

WHO WERE FOOTBALL'S FINEST?

2 In a city dominated by its love for baseball, St. Louis is fortunate enough to have witnessed some remarkable football stars ply their trades. If we did this list 5 or 10 years from now, the NFL would undoubtedly have a larger presence on this list of St. Louis greats. But for now, the list is a tight and celebrated group of beloved and well-respected men who pack Hall of Fame credentials or (at least in one case) mercurial celebrity.

4. DAN DIERDORF

Although fans of the football Cardinals didn't have much to be excited about, Dan Dierdorf was a member of the old Big Red who made his mark in pro football on and off the field.

One of the game's most outstanding offensive linemen, Dierdorf was inducted into the NFL Hall of Fame in 1996 after a 13-year career with the football Cardinals. He was an All-American at the University of Michigan before joining the Cardinals in 1971 as a second-round draft pick. Dierdorf was a member of one of the best offensive lines in NFL history, one that permitted the fewest sacks in the NFC for five straight years in the mid-1970s. In 1975, the Cardinals set a then-record by allowing only eight sacks in 14 games.

Dierdorf was more than a football player. After retiring from football, he became one of the most popular network television broadcasters, spending more than a decade on *Monday Night Football*.

3. LARRY WILSON

Old-school pro football lovers will certify that if you're going to designate only one member of the old football Cardinals for St. Louis sports immortality, safety Larry Wilson is that man.

Wilson belongs on this list because he helped redefine the safety position, popularizing the safety blitz in his 13 seasons in the NFL, all with Big Red. A ferocious hitter and a ball hawk, Wilson had 52 career interceptions. During one stretch he picked off at least one pass in seven straight games. He was in eight Pro Bowls and named All-NFL six times.

Wilson's toughness made him popular with fans of the Big Red. He was only 6 feet tall and barely 190 pounds, but when he came in on those blitzes, quarterbacks knew they

19

were going to get thumped. Likewise, receivers knew that when they came across the middle it was wise to look out for Wilson. He once played a game with casts on both his hands—and still picked off a pass.

2. KURT WARNER

If songwriter Paul Simon had ever been a devoted Rams fan, Kurt Warner would have surely been the inspiration for some memorable lyric that elevated the quarterback to hero status. In these odd and turbulent times of flawed, defrocked, and dishonorable sports stars, Warner is the embodiment of the songwriter's romantic longing for rare and unassailable sports heroes.

The former Rams quarterback was like a modern-day Joe DiMaggio. For much of his brief but shining five seasons with the Rams, St. Louis turned its lonely eyes toward him. Warner gave this town a ton: a Super Bowl victory, two NFL MVP awards, and arguably the three best years any passer had in NFL history.

But even more importantly, he was a genuine Christian soldier, a philanthropist, a media-friendly superstar and down-to-earth human being who never forgot his roots or took for granted his unusual rise to fame and fortune from a grocery store stock clerk to an NFL superstar.

In the end, he also gave us a soap opera craziness that divided the entire town and forced every Rams loyalist to choose sides. In those final, injury-plagued seasons in St.

Louis, this city was split into two definitive camps—pro-Warner or pro-Marc Bulger. While Bulger quickly took over as the starter in 2002 and became a Pro Bowler, Warner was sent out of town in 2004, spending the last few years of his career as an unhappy backup to a series of rookie No. 1 draft picks.

But St. Louis will always remember him most for the good times, when Warner thrilled everyone in his role as ringmaster of the Greatest Show on Turf. Now that the glorious ride is over, we ought to pause for a long moment and rightfully give props to one of the finest guys to ever hitch a ride on the magic carpet from rags to riches.

1. MARSHALL FAULK

The athletic genius of Marshall Faulk is that he was somehow able to combine football's artful aesthetic, brutish violence, and high-minded intelligence into a Hall of Fame-caliber game.

Roll back over Faulk's career highlight reel and you'll surely smile at the sight of that uncanny, stop-on-a-dime jump cut in the open field that always made him appear to be the elegant matador, while his flailing defender was the snorting, foolishly overmatched bull. You'll also find a little package of thunder in there, too, sticking his shoulder into the collapsing gut of an on-rushing blitzing linebacker or pass-rushing defensive end who outweighed him by 50 to 80 pounds in order to keep Kurt Warner safe from harm's way.

Or perhaps it was the signature blur of his wiggling shoulders, quick-shuffling feet, and fast-twitch eyes scanning the field, all in perfect synchronization, as Faulk slipped through that ever-so-slight slash of light and galloped into the open field.

But never forget the most important aspect of the essential Marshall Faulk. For all the delight that the graceful Marshall, the elusive Marshall, the physical Marshall provided, there is one equally significant component that made No. 28 one of the greatest all-around offensive weapons in the modern NFL. We can call it "Fundamental Faulk."

Wind back the highlight reel to 1999, midway through his first season with the Rams. The team was on its way to a magical Super Bowl trip, but this was one of the three games they would lose along the way, a 3-point defeat October 31 at the hands of the Tennessee Titans in Nashville.

In the closing moments of the game, when the Rams were scrambling to make a comeback, Warner completed a short pass over the middle to Az-Zahir Hakim. The moment the little receiver caught the ball, he was popped by a Titans defender and fell to the ground woozy and totally disoriented. The clock was ticking. Hakim tried to get up, but was in so much pain he collapsed on his back again. Out of nowhere, Faulk ran up to Hakim, grabbed him underneath his shoulder pads, and pulled him to his feet.

"And in that moment, we saw the definitive example of what kind of leader Marshall is," Warner told me a few months after that game. "We had no timeouts left, and Az is completely out of it, and Marshall realized it and knew exactly what to do."

Faulk had the presence of mind to drag Hakim to the line of scrimmage, literally shoving him where he was supposed to be in the formation. He told him the play, then jumped back into the slot so the Rams were able to get the play off without a penalty.

"You didn't see anybody else on the team going to pick Az up," linebacker London Fletcher said. "That just right there showed me what kind of student of the game [he was] and how knowledgeable he was about the game."

Lots of great athletes have come and gone with pure athleticism equal to or superior to Faulk. But few have ever entered the NFL with Faulk's uncanny blend of athletic style and football intelligence. If there's any justice, Faulk ought to ride the express lane into the Pro Football Hall of Fame.

We often do a great injustice to athletic legends. We assume that these extraordinary athletes become Hall of Fame caliber by merely being born as extraordinary physical specimens. We should know better. The truly great ones separate themselves from the rest of the pack because they work harder and study longer. The minute you met Marshall Faulk, you found out he was one of those dedicated, hard-working geniuses.

Faulk's brilliance wasn't only formed in the bright sunlight on those back fields at the Rams' practice facility.

It was cultivated long after the sun had gone down in the near-empty meeting rooms. Former Rams offensive line coach Jim Hanifan loves telling stories about Faulk and how he would often walk into Hanny's office or in a meeting room on countless quiet days and nights when the only sound in the Rams Park hallways was the whirl and click of game tapes running through VCRs.

"He'd come in and sit down and just start picking my brain," Hanifan said. "This guy would be in there with me and he'd want to know everything [the offensive line] was doing. He wanted to not only know what we were doing, but why we were doing it."

The legendary coach would smile when he told Faulk tales, and he usually ended them all the same way. "You wanna know why Marshall's so good?" he'd ask. "Smartest bleepin' guy in the room, that's why. Smartest bleepin' guy."

As good as Kurt Warner was, and despite those league MVP awards, inside the Rams locker room Faulk was always considered the *team MVP*. When history ultimately records who the most significant football player in St. Louis was (hmm, I guess we're doing that right now, aren't we?), the evidence will be overwhelming that Faulk was the best. He was a game-changer at his position, the key athlete and team leader throughout the Greatest Show era.

He was the missing link in the Rams evolution from also-ran to Super Bowl winners. That makes him the best there ever was.

WHO WERE THE BEST BLUES?

3 Even though the Blues have never won the Stanley Cup, their lack of championships has not resulted in a lack of fan passion. St. Louis fell in love with many of its hockey greats. These are the ones who deserve the most notoriety.

3. AL MacINNIS

He is not the greatest Blue of all time, but he might be the most beloved. Al MacInnis, who was elected into the Hockey Hall of Fame in his first year of eligibility in June of 2007, deserves his place among St. Louis sports royalty. He played 23 NHL seasons, including 10 with the Blues.

The seven-time All-Star defenseman won a Norris Trophy with the Blues (1999) and was one of the greatest all-time goal scorers among defensemen (his 1,274 points scored and his career 340 goals rank third all-time among defensemen). He arrived in St. Louis via a 1997 trade with the Calgary Flames, where he won a Stanley Cup and the Conn Smythe (playoff MVP) Trophy. But most hockey folks believe MacInnis earned his Hall of Fame reputation in his years with the Blues. He trails only Ray Bourque and Paul Coffey in goals, assists, and points all-time for an NHL defenseman.

MacInnis solidified his standing with St. Louis sports fans by retiring here, raising his family here, then returning to the Blues front office to help general manager John Davidson rebuild the franchise from the rubble left by former owner Bill Laurie's dismantling of the roster.

2. BERNIE FEDERKO

Bernie Federko was elected to the Hockey Hall of Fame in 2002, yet he has always been overlooked quite a bit as a great player in Blues history. He wasn't as popular as teammate Brian Sutter, whose obvious hard-charging style was more to the fans' tastes. As a result, they often missed out on Federko's subtle creativity. And of course, he then got lost in the glow of Brett Hull's enormous star power when the "Golden Brett" glamorized hockey for St. Louis.

If they had an award for "most reliable Blue," Federko would get it every time. But flashy? Colorful? Glamorous? No, that was never Federko. In 1986, in a poll conducted by *GOAL* magazine, he was named the most overlooked talent in hockey.

We do tend to gloss over the importance of what Federko did (scoring 100 points in a season four times; topping 90 points in seven of eight seasons between 1978 and 1986). Federko epitomized what it was to be a consistent but constantly overlooked star, even while becoming the first player in NHL history to collect at least 50 assists in 10 straight seasons. That gift just didn't register with hockey fans in the high-scoring era of Wayne Gretzky, who was scoring 200 points a season.

Federko retired with 369 goals and 761 assists for 1,130 points in 1,000 NHL games. Although his 1.13 points per game alone might be enough for admission to the Hall of Fame, Federko did so much more and meant so much more to the Blues and their fans.

What will always keep Federko close to Blues fans' hearts and souls is his loyalty to the franchise and the city. He could have left St. Louis and gone on to gain greater fame in his sport. He had good reason to leave many times, considering how many bad ownership groups tried to run the Blues into the ground during his early years here. Yet Federko chose to play the first 13 years of his 14-year NHL career here.

Blues fans will always hold him in high regard for that.

1. BRETT HULL

No list of St. Louis favorites could be complete without Brett Hull, who *is* St. Louis hockey. The day he arrived in town to play for the Blues, there were no more than four ice skating rinks in town. Now there are more than 30. His influence as the first popular hockey superstar spawned a wave of future NHL players from St. Louis hockey rinks and youth leagues.

The "Golden Brett" is one of the most influential figures in St. Louis sports because he almost single-handedly turned St. Louis into a true hockey town. In his 11 seasons here, Hull became one of the most popular players we've ever had. A Hull Blues sweater was a mandatory part of athletic gear for a true St. Louis fan, just as much as a Cardinals cap or jersey.

Hull currently holds the all-time Blues franchise record in goals (527), hat tricks (27), game-winning goals (70), power play goals (195), and shots on goal (3,367). Furthermore, he ranks second in assists (409), points (936), and shorthanded goals (18). He broke the Blues all-time record for goals in a season with 72 in 1989–90. The following season, Hull shattered his own mark by scoring 86 goals, the third most in NHL history and the most ever by a right winger. In the same season, he scored 50 goals in 49 games, becoming the first Blue to score 50 goals in 50 games or less.

Hull won the Hart Trophy as the NHL's MVP while a Blue. In 1991–92 he became the second player in NHL history to score 50 goals in 50 games twice, as well as the second player in history to record 70-plus goals in three consecutive seasons. In 1993–94, Hull scored 57 goals, marking his fifth consecutive season with 50 or more.

WHO WERE THE BEST IN BASKETBALL?

4 The hockey loyalists are now in a snit. Wait a minute, how can basketball have more men on this list of all-time greats than hockey? Well, that's easy. Legends pull rank. Some of the hockey guys who were left off this all-time list lost out in the voting to basketball guys because of their place in their sport's overall history. This group includes two Top 50 all-time greats in NBA history, not to mention a college and pro great in St. Louis, and one man who is in the Hall of Fame as a coach after being an All-American as a player.

4. NORM STEWART

First as an outstanding All-America player, then later as a Hall of Fame coach, Norm Stewart became a Missouri basketball legend, someone who belongs in any conversation about significant St. Louis sports figures.

On his coaching alone, Stewart ranks as one of the best in the business. He ran the Mizzou basketball program for 32 seasons, compiling a 634–333 overall mark. With a career record of 731 victories over 38 seasons, Stewart is slated to be inducted into the inaugural 11-member class of the National Collegiate Basketball Hall of Fame on November 18, 2007, in Kansas City.

To understand how high the basketball community regards Stewart's hoop legacy, all you need to do is look at the company he's keeping in that initial class for the Hall of Fame: Kareem Abdul Jabbar, Phog Allen, Adolph Rupp, Henry Iba, John McLendon, Charles "Lefty" Driesell, Guy Lewis, Austin Carr, Dick Groat, Dick Barnett, and Vic Bubbas.

By the time he retired in 1999, Stewart ranked No. 7 on college basketball's all-time wins list. Only two coaches had coached in more career games than the 1,106 Stewart directed during his coaching tenure. Stewart's coaching résumé is loaded with honors:

- Stewart was voted the Big Eight Conference's All-Time Coach by both the Associated Press and the *Kansas City Star.*
- He led Mizzou to 8 Big Eight Conference championships and 6 conference tournament crowns.
- He produced 28 first team all-league picks, 8 first-team All-Americans, and 29 NBA draft picks.
- He was named National Coach of the Year in 1982 and 1994.
- He was named the Big Eight Conference's Coach of the Year five times.
- He was District Coach of the Year seven times.

As an athlete, Stewart was a three-time letterman in two sports (basketball and baseball), led the Tigers in scoring in 1956 with a 24.1 point average, and played in the Baltimore Orioles minor league organization, as well as part of one season with the NBA St. Louis Hawks.

3. LENNY WILKENS

Lenny Wilkens began his pro basketball career in St. Louis inauspiciously, with an owner who: (1.) didn't want to draft him, (2.) immediately tried to get the general manager to dump him during rookie camp, and (3.) protested angrily when the rookie point guard was finally put into the starting lineup early in his first season with the Hawks.

But Ben Kerner's ignorance of basketball talent did not stop Wilkens from enjoying a long and honored Hall of Fame career as one of the 50 greatest players in NBA history. In that rookie 1960 season, in which the owner was convinced Wilkens couldn't play, he dished out enough assists to have three teammates score more than 20 points a game (Bob Pettit with a 27.9 average, and fellow future Hall of Famers Cliff Hagan with a 22.1. average and Clyde Lovellette with 22.0), as the Hawks finished with the best record in franchise history (51–28), won the division and conference title, and reached the NBA finals.

In his eight seasons in St. Louis, Wilkens helped lead the Hawks to eight consecutive playoff appearances, three division titles, six conference finals, and two trips to the NBA finals. His last season in St. Louis, 1968, was his best: He averaged 20 points, 8.3 assists, and 5.3 rebounds, while the Hawks improved their franchise record for regular-season victories to 56 and reached the Western Conference finals.

Even more achievements would follow for Wilkens after leaving the Hawks. He would go on to become the winningest coach in NBA history, and was voted into the Hall of Fame in 1989.

All and all, not a bad career for a slender kid from the streets of Brooklyn, New York, who almost got cut as a rookie.

2. ED MACAULEY

Greg Marecek, author of *Full Court: The Untold Stories of the St. Louis Hawks*, and a noted hoop historian, believes that "Mr. St. Louis Basketball" is without question the man known as "Easy Ed" Macauley.

Born and raised in St. Louis, Macauley was a high school star (at St. Louis U High), a college star, a pro All-Star, and a championship coach. In fact, there isn't much Macauley didn't do in the basketball world. Macauley is the most celebrated and decorated basketball player to ever come out of a St. Louis high school. He was a two-time collegiate All-American and National Player of the Year who led St. Louis University to the 1948 National Invitation Tournament title, which back then was considered the collegiate national championship.

He earned his famous nickname "Easy Ed" during his freshman year at SLU, when it was his turn to be captain for a game. The Billikens that year rotated captains every game, and on the night it was Macauley's turn, he was extremely nervous—so nervous, in fact, that the head coach tried to settle him down.

His coach told him his only job as team captain was to lead the team out of the locker room and onto the gym floor for pregame drills. So the big freshman excitedly pushed the door open and ran out onto the floor, dribbled the ball, and took several shots before he noticed that none of his teammates had followed him onto the floor...because the band was playing the National Anthem.

Macauley was so nervous, he never heard the music.

Now the fans were yelling at him, laughing at him, telling him, "Hey, take it easy, Ed." In the commotion, the school's publicity man Warren Netwin heard what the fans said, liked the ring of "Easy Ed," and began putting it in his press releases. The nickname stuck and a legend was born.

Macauley became the most significant player in SLU history when he took the Billikens to that national title in 1948, then moved on to the professional ranks to become a six-time NBA All-Star with the Boston Celtics.

Yet in the basketball history books, Macauley's celebrity must also include the fact that he was on the wrong side of the most important trade in NBA history, when the St. Louis Hawks sent Boston the draft rights to a rookie out of the University of San Francisco named Bill Russell for "Easy Ed" and Cliff Hagan in 1956.

33

After returning to St. Louis as a pro, Macauley only played two more full seasons before taking over as the Hawks head coach, leading them to two division titles and two trips to the Western Conference finals. His career winning percentage as a coach was .650 (89–48). One year after retiring as a player and coach, he was inducted into the Basketball Hall of Fame.

1. BOB PETTIT

While Macauley may have been "Mr. St. Louis Basketball," Marecek calls Bob "Big Blue" Pettit the greatest Hawk ever. Unless you are over 50, you probably have no idea just how impressive a basketball player Bob Pettit was. Although his last season was 1965, the greatest basketball player to ever hoop it up in St. Louis would have been great no matter the era in which he played.

Pettit had career averages of 26.4 points and 16.2 rebounds, was a two-time NBA MVP, and a first-team All-NBA selection for 10 consecutive seasons. But he will always be known for leading the Hawks to their only NBA title in 1958 and breaking up, at least momentarily, the vaunted Boston Celtics domination of pro basketball. The high point of that series was when he scored 50 points in the decisive sixth game of the NBA finals.

Pettit was named one of the 50 greatest players in NBA history, and there's no doubt he deserved it. He was a big, strong scoring and rebounding machine. For the younger sports fan, think of him like Karl Malone, another Louisiana boy with a passion for playing in the paint.

One of the biggest shames of losing the Hawks in 1968 was how St. Louis abandoned any thought of remembering the franchise's greatness and the man who led them to so many victories, "Big Blue." With Pettit, the Hawks were the second best team of their era behind the dynastic Celtics. From 1956 through Pettit's final year in pro ball (1965), the Hawks reached the NBA finals four times, reached the conference finals eight times, won five division titles, and reached the playoffs all nine years.

There should be a statue in Pettit's honor somewhere in the city, but pro basketball is a distant memory in St. Louis, so consider this a healthy reminder of Bob Pettit's greatness.

WHO ARE THE BEST OF THE REST?

5 Not all the best and most notable figures in our city's sports history played the major sports. Some actually never played at all. Who are these folks and where do they rank in our hearts and minds? Here's the best of the rest.

5. THE SPINKS BROTHERS

Leon and Michael Spinks are the first family of boxing in St. Louis. In the 1976 Montreal Olympics, the Spinks brothers became the first brothers to win Gold Medals in the same Olympic sport in the same year, as well as the first brothers to become professional heavyweight champions.

After the Olympics, Michael, the middleweight Gold Medalist, temporarily quit boxing, taking a night shift job as a janitor at a Monsanto plant. Leon, the heavyweight Gold Medalist, immediately turned professional. It didn't take Michael long to forget about being a janitor—he fell asleep one night on the job and was fired—as he became a pro less than a year after the Montreal Games. When he started his professional career, Michael quickly moved up in weight class, starting as a light heavyweight, and then moving to the more lucrative heavyweight division.

The gap-toothed Leon grabbed quick international fame when he pulled off a shocking upset of the legendary world heavyweight champion Muhammad Ali in a 1978 title bout, and he became the heavyweight champ in only his eighth professional fight. He didn't stay on top very long, because seven months later Leon faced Ali again and lost. He became the shortest reigning heavyweight champ in boxing history, and earned more fame for his toothless grin and the continuous troubles he ran into out of the ring.

Michael Spinks took a more patient path to the top of the pro ranks. After running his record as a light heavyweight to 17–0, he won the World Boxing Association Light Heavyweight Title in a 1981 victory over Eddie Mustafa Muhammad, then defended his title five times. Four years later, he moved up to the heavyweight division, and just like his brother, he pulled off an upset of another great champion, 48–0 Larry Holmes, in a 15-round title match. Michael held onto the belt until a 90-second first-round KO at the hands of a young Mike Tyson in 1988.

4. JIMMY CONNORS

"I hate to lose more than I love to win."

If you ever saw Jimmy Connors play tennis, you understood how much this famous quote defined his entire athletic life. The feisty, colorful, and combative Connors dominated men's tennis in the 1970s with his talent and his personality.

"I want to bring the crowd into the match," Connors once said. "In short, turn it into a football game." And that's what he did every time he stepped onto the court, revving up the crowd and getting them to love him or hate him.

Born across the Mississippi River from St. Louis in Bellville, Illinois, on September 2, 1952, young Jimmy Connors quickly fell in love with tennis thanks to his mother, Gloria, a local teaching pro, and his grandmother, Bertha Thompson. He had a racquet in his hand when he was a toddler, and became a local star in youth tennis. Ultimately, he rose to the top of the tennis world, reaching the world No. 1 ranking in July of 1974, then holding onto the top spot for 160 straight weeks. Over the course of his career, Connors was ranked No. 1 in the world for a total of 268 weeks.

There wasn't much Connors didn't accomplish in his long career, winning five U.S Open titles, two Wimbledons, and one Australian Open. For five consecutive years in the 1970s, the left-handed champion ended the year ranked No. 1.

3. MIKE SHANNON

"Even the standing-room-only seats have been sold."

He is not quite the elegant wordsmith of his old broadcast

buddy and legendary voice, the late Jack Buck, but there is no doubt that Mike Shannon belongs among the most notable sports figures in St. Louis history. As a high school athlete at Christian Brothers College, he was a standout football, basketball, and baseball player. At Missouri, he was a scholarship quarterback with so much promise that if he stayed in Columbia, he would have been a Heisman Trophy candidate.

If you talk to old-school St. Louis sports fans, most will tell you that Shannon was one of the greatest, if not *the* greatest, high school athlete to ever come through the city.

He was a key member of those great Cardinals teams in the 1960s, with a nine-year major league career and a lifetime .255 batting average.

But come on now, that's not really why he's on this list, is it?

"Jack, it's great to see those ivory-colored walls again here at Wrigley Field."

Shannon is the ultimate St. Louis baseball wise guy/bon vivant and lovable king of the city. What most people in St. Louis believe is that he could drive his car out into center field at Busch Stadium, spin his wheels in tight circles, then park it on the warning track, and no one would say a word.

Ahh, but speaking of words, aren't words what Mike Shannon's all about?

39

"They'll be hanging from the roofters in Shea when the Cardinals come to town."

No one in the history of St. Louis sports who earned a living in a broadcast booth has managed to come up with more signature phrases and comical faux pas than the syrupy voiced Shannon.

"They got a guy named Diaz (pronounced "die-az") and we got a Diaz (pronounced "dee-ez"), and they're both spelled the same. I tell you folks, English is a strange language."

Trying to come up with the definitive list of "Shannonisms" is impossible. There isn't enough time or space in this book to adequately capture the ultimate wacky moments that Shannon has provided for us on those steamy St. Louis summer days and nights. It begins with that familiar "Heeh, heehhh, heehhh" cackle that lights up the air waves, rolls smoothly to his "Steeeee-rike!" call, then crescendoes with his "Get up, baby, get up!" home run call. But most of all, what endears him to everyone is his unusual grasp of the English language, providing countless moments of unique entertainment opportunities.

Shannon: "I've heard that if you know English, Spanish, Italian, and I think it's French, you can go just about anywhere in this world... except for China, where they have all of those derelicts."

Jack Buck: "Do you mean 'dialects'?"

Shannon: "Yeah, dialects, that's what I mean. But they got a lot of derelicts, too!"

Well of course they do, Mike. And we always know exactly what you mean, and we love every minute of your nightly linguistic adventures.

2. JACKIE JOYNER-KERSEE

Jackie Joyner-Kersee, the queen of American track and field, came out of East St. Louis to rise in international prominence as one of the most significant figures in Olympic track history, and is rightfully considered one of the finest all-around athletes ever.

Sports Illustrated named her the greatest female athlete of the 20th century, yet to me she was more than that. She was one of the finest all-around athletes I ever saw, period.

She was a world-class level performer in the heptathlon (she holds the world record and six of the all-time greatest marks in heptathlon history). She was one of the greatest long jumpers in the history of her event and was world-ranked as a 100-meter hurdler and 200-meter sprinter, plus she was good enough to earn a basketball scholarship at UCLA.

The five-time Olympic medalist (three Gold, one Silver, one Bronze) was also one of the most gracious international ambassadors to sports you'll ever meet. And somehow, this sweet and gracious lady was also one of the toughest competitors I ever saw. It didn't matter if she was in pain because of a strained muscle, or if her asthma was restricting her breathing in an important competition. Jackie Joyner-Kersee found a way to will herself to victory.

1. JACK BUCK

"That's a winner!"

You don't have to wonder why a radio and television broadcaster like Jack Buck is on this list of the most notable names in St. Louis sports history. Without swinging a bat, throwing a pitch, shooting a jump shot, or scoring a touchdown, Jack Buck was as deeply engrained in the sports fabric of St. Louis as anyone else on this list of athletic legends.

What Jack Buck gave St. Louis transcends what happened on the field of play. Buck gave us the most memorable phrases and mental portraits of our baseball days and nights. He took us through childhood, talked to us in our cars and basements, gave us our Cardinals history, and retold all our favorite baseball stories.

"Smith corks one into deep right field, down the line. It may go.... Go crazy, folks! Go crazy! It's a home run and the Cardinals have won the game 3–2, on a home run by the Wizard!"

You could measure your baseball life by his famous calls and phrases. Every summer night he welcomed Cardinals Nation to another fellowship service with the most comforting words of any St. Louis summer evening:

"Good evening everybody, welcome to Cardinals baseball."

Think about where you were and what you were doing when the greatest moments in baseball history occurred, then remember that Jack was there, too, capturing the moment in his own precise and poetic way:

"Unbelievable! The Dodgers have won the game on a home run by Kirk Gibson! I don't believe what I just saw!"

The voice of Jack Buck was Cardinals baseball. Actually, his voice was more than that. It was the rich and romantic voice of an entire sport. He introduced you to Gibson and Brock, rhapsodized about Ozzie and Big Mac, chatted with Hammerin' Hank, Willie, and Mickey. He was an essential character in the colorful past of Cardinals baseball. On the day of his tearful memorial in old Busch Stadium in June of

2002, his son Joe captured best what Jack Buck meant to St. Louis and why he deserves to be on this notable list:

> *"We are thankful to God for the bat of Musial, for the arm of Gibson, for the legs of Brock, for the power of McGwire. We are all here today to say thank you to God for Jack Buck."*

He came to us at the beginning of talk radio, on KMOX's "At Your Service," swept right through the golden era of baseball radio broadcasting, then shifted seamlessly into the modern era of TV and radio without a hitch. He fought in World War II, and was the comforting and emotional voice after 9/11 that reminded us how strong we still were as a nation.

So before you ask me "What's some broadcaster doing on this list?" all I will tell you is, "He's not *some broadcaster*. He's Jack Buck!"

THE GOOD, BAD, AND UGLY

St. Louis is a town rich in historic sports moments, many of them good, some of them bad, others peculiar, fascinating, and frustrating. Let's take a look at the best, worst, and most shameful, dramatic, and significant events in the city's sports history.

WHAT WAS THE WORST DECISION IN ST. LOUIS SPORTS HISTORY?

6 There have been more than a fair share of rotten decisions made concerning sports in St. Louis over the years, such as three pro franchises (the Browns, the Hawks, and the football Cardinals) abandoning St. Louis; the annual idiotic first-round picks of the Grid Birds; the Rams selecting Lawrence Phillips; and the silly notion that Mike Martz thought he could win a Super Bowl without giving the ball to Marshall Faulk.

However, nothing rises to the level of the preposterous mistake St. Louis Hawks owner Ben Kerner committed. In the formative years of the Hawks franchise, financially strapped owner Kerner had two chances to turn his fledgling NBA team into one of the greatest in league history. He could have had Red Auerbach as his coach and Bill Russell as the team's cornerstone player.

Yet within a span of seven years, Kerner gave away Auerbach and Russell to the Boston Celtics, forever altering the history of pro basketball. The Celtics would become the most dominant franchise in pro basketball history, and the Hawks would leave St. Louis. How'd it happen?

During the 1948–49 season of the old National Basketball League, Kerner kept trying to fix his Tri-Cities Hawks (a precursor to the St. Louis NBA franchise). But Kerner didn't really know as much about the game as he thought he did, and his meddlesome ways were a constant thorn in the side of his young coach, who grew tired of hearing the owner complain and give him lineup ultimatums.

That young coach was Arnold "Red" Auerbach.

At the end of the 28–29 season, the NBL and the old Basketball Association of America merged to form what is now the National Basketball Association. As part of the merger, Kerner gladly agreed to a league request to send the fiery young coach to the Boston Celtics, so he fired him to let him out of his contract and free him up for Boston.

Ouch.

Things would get worse for Kerner and his Hawks. He had moved the team from the tri-cities (Davenport, Iowa, and Rock Island and Moline, Illinois) to Milwaukee with little financial success. So in 1955, Kerner moved the franchise again, this time to St. Louis, for the 1955–56 season.

At the end of that dismal season, the Hawks ended up with the No. 2 overall pick in the NBA draft. For some inexplicable reason the Rochester Royals, who owned the first pick, skipped over the NCAA champion University of San Francisco's 6-foot-11 center William Fenton Russell, and instead selected Sihugo Green, the All-American out of Duquesne.

The Celtics, led by the young coach Auerbach, arranged a trade with Kerner for the rights to the second pick. Auerbach gave up former St. Louis University All-American and NBA All-Star forward "Easy Ed" Macauley and another star guard, Cliff Hagan, for the draft rights to Russell.

While Hagan and Macauley would end up leading the Hawks to the 1958 NBA title, on their way to the Basketball Hall of Fame, Russell would become one of the greatest players in the history of the game. His pairing with the coaching genius Auerbach would lead the Celtics to a staggering 12 NBA titles. A 12-time NBA All-Star, Russell would go on to win five league MVPs in his star-studded career.

And just think, all of that could have happened in St. Louis.

WHAT WAS THE SINGLE MOST SIGNIFICANT MOMENT IN ST. LOUIS SPORTS HISTORY?

7 It started off innocently enough, with a simple trade and a brief phone call. On October 8, 1969, at the conclusion of the 1969 season, St. Louis Cardinals assistant general manager Jim Toomey placed a two-minute phone call to star center fielder Curt Flood to inform him that the team had just traded him and teammates Tim McCarver, Joe Hoerner, and Byron Browne to the Philadelphia Phillies for Richie Allen, Cookie Rojas, and Jerry Johnson.

No one could have imagined at that moment that the world of professional sports was on the verge of being significantly altered. The Cards' attempt to trade Flood was the beginning of a series of events that would begin to launch the free agency era in sports.

Flood believed that baseball's restrictive reserve clause, which kept him in the service of his original team even after the contract expired, was unfair to players and akin to modern-day slavery. No matter how badly a player desired to pick and choose where he wanted to play, he could not freely move to another team without his original team's consent. So Flood refused to report to the Phillies and on Christmas Eve wrote a letter to Commissioner Bowie Kuhn that would change the face of sports forever:

"December 24, 1969

"After twelve years in the major leagues, I do not feel I am a piece of property to be bought and sold irrespective of my wishes. I believe that any system which produces that result violates my basic rights as a citizen and is inconsistent with the laws of the United States and of the several States.

"It is my desire to play baseball in 1970, and I am capable of playing. I have received a contract offer from the Philadelphia club, but I believe I have the right to consider offers from other clubs before making any decision. I, therefore, request that you make known to all Major League clubs my feelings in this matter, and advise them of my availability for the 1970 season."

While Flood demanded that Kuhn declare him a free agent, Kuhn refused, citing the reserve clause in his Cardinals contract. So Flood consulted with Players Association head Marvin Miller, who said the union would support him in any legal action against Major League Baseball.

A month later, Flood filed a $4.1 million lawsuit against Kuhn and Major League Baseball, claiming that baseball was violating federal antitrust laws with the reserve clause. The case *Flood v. Kuhn* divided baseball's inner circle, with active players taking both Flood and the owners' sides and splitting the heart of the game for several turbulent years. The landmark case eventually went to the Supreme Court, and eventually favored the owners by a 5–3 margin. Flood was traded to the Washington Senators, received a raise to $110,000, and eventually retired.

But the case put something powerful into motion. In 1975 an arbitrator struck down the reserve clause when Peter Seitz ruled that pitchers Andy Messersmith and Dave McNally had played one season without a contract, which gave them free agent status, and so the "Flood-gates" to free agency were swung wide open, and pro sports was never the same.

WHAT WAS THE MOST HISTORIC MOMENT IN ST. LOUIS SPORTS HISTORY?

8 At the turn of the 21st century, St. Louis was readily identified as a pass-crazy football town. With the emergence of the Rams' high-octane "Greatest Show on Turf" offense, the Rams attack could easily produce 300- and 400-yard passing displays by quarterback Kurt Warner and his amazing arsenal of deep threat receivers, as well as through the skills of multitalented running back Marshall Faulk.

At the turn of the 20th century, St. Louis was acknowledged as the actual birthplace of the forward pass. Only a few miles west of the future site of the Edward Jones Dome, St. Louis University head football coach Eddie Cochems became the innovator of the forward pass on a practice field on the SLU campus. He had initially hatched the forward pass during a two-month-long training camp in Lake Beulah, Wisconsin, then perfected it at practice in St. Louis, dubbing it the "overhead projectile spiral pass." He told the student magazine the *Fleur de Lis*, "I think that the ...pass will develop many beautiful spectacular plays before the season closes."

Until 1906, college football was an overly violent game full of dangerous tactics. In the 1905 season, the *Chicago Tribune* reported that 18 college football players had died and 159 had been seriously injured as a result of collisions during games. After the 1905 season, several major universities dropped football, calling it a "boy-killing, man-mutilating sport."

During two meetings in December 1905 and January of 2006, the precursor to the NCAA met and began to overhaul the rules of football. One rule was allowing the ball to progress downfield by means of the forward pass. Until

1906, there were occasions when players illegally threw the ball and were usually penalized for it.

It didn't take Cochems long to practice what he preached. On September 5, 1906, in a game at Carroll (Wisconsin) College, all his rehearsals paid off when quarterback Bradbury Robinson flung the first legal forward pass. His first attempt failed, but on his second toss, he connected with receiver Jack Schneider for a touchdown in a 22–0 rout.

Sadly for both Cochems and Robinson, American sports mythology did not give them much credit for their innovation. Neither man was ever elected into the college football Hall of Fame, and the sports movie classic *Knute Rockne: All-American* popularized the false notion that the first forward pass was completed in a 1913 game between Notre Dame and Army, when Irish quarterback Gus Dorais completed a strike to Rockne in a 35–13 victory over Army's mighty Black Knights.

Nearly 100 years later, a white-haired football eccentric named Mike Martz stood in front of a chalkboard and started designing high-tech Xs and Os, launching the Rams' "Greatest Show on Turf" that would revolutionize the way pro football was played: an aggressive, take-no-prisoners style of offense that lit up the scoreboard like a video game.

Somewhere, Eddie Cochems was smiling.

WHAT WAS THE MOST CONTROVERSIAL MOMENT IN ST. LOUIS SPORTS HISTORY?

9 This moment is not so much a local legend as it is an uncertain and conflicting alleged crime. Did several members of the St. Louis Cardinals get together and attempt to organize a league-wide player boycott of Jackie Robinson during his historic 1947 season, when he signed with the Brooklyn Dodgers and became the first black player in modern major league history? It depends on who you talk to and which newspaper's version you prefer to believe.

In early May, 1947, reports out of New York surfaced that several unnamed St. Louis Cardinals had hatched a plan to conduct an organized strike against Robinson. *New York Herald Tribune* sports editor Stanley Woodward wrote that the Cardinals (most likely led by Harry Walker in St. Louis, and urged by the grumbling of Robinson's Brooklyn teammate Dixie Walker, Harry's brother) were prepared to sit out the first Cards–Dodgers game in Brooklyn on May 6.

However, when club owner Sam Breadon got wind of the

alleged plan, Breadon flew to New York to meet with the players, then had a meeting with National League president Ford Frick. After the meeting, the two men joined forces to emphatically quash the walkout. According to Woodward's famous article, Frick issued this stern rebuke of the players:

"If you do this you will be suspended from the league. You will find that the friends you think you have in the press box will not support you, that you will be outcasts. I do not care if the league strikes. Those who do it will encounter quick retribution. They will be suspended, and I don't care if it wrecks the National League for five years. This is the United States of America, and one citizen has as much right to play as another."

In the days after the Herald Tribune story became public, Cardinals players and officials denied the story in the *St. Louis Post–Dispatch*, *Globe Democrat*, and several New York newspapers. In addition, closer examination of Woodward's story revealed that it had some factual holes. According to best-selling author Jonathan Eig, who wrote a book chronicling Robinson's historic first season called *Opening Day*, it was unclear just how much of that story Woodward embellished. "From the interviews and research I uncovered—including an unpublished interview with Frick several years later—it's clear that something did happen, but maybe not quite like Woodward described," Eig told me. "Ford Frick did admit that he said something to Breadon about (the alleged boycott), but not exactly what Woodward said he told the players."

Whatever the facts, within 24 hours the story swept around the country, and nearly the entire Cardinals team was branded as a bunch of bigots. One of the only Cardinals to come out of the story looking good was Stan Musial. "The Man" came home from the road trip with a case of "appendicitis." In the days after the May 9 story broke, a story floated around that Musial's stomach ailment was the result of a rumored brawl with teammate Enos "Country" Slaughter because Musial refused to join in the boycott.

Musial to this day denies there was a fight, and says there was no planned protest. In an interview several years ago with writer Roger Kahn, however, Musial admitted that he heard teammates talk, although he never took it seriously.

Perhaps the best explanation for what happened comes from Eig: "From what I was able to discover, what likely happened was that there were some players who were mad, and they shot off their mouths. Was there an organized protest planned? It's hard to say. Breadon definitely talked to Frick, and Frick definitely told Breadon to deliver a message to the players. Was it the message that Woodward wrote in his story? No, it probably wasn't. There's also no doubt that some white [sports writers] were interested in minimizing the story, too. Was it because they didn't get the story first, or was it because they were protecting the players who were their friends? Or did Woodward spring from the pack and exaggerate the story for impact? That is the thing I guess we'll never really know."

WHAT WAS THE MOST DRAMATIC MOMENT IN MODERN ST. LOUIS BASEBALL HISTORY?

10. Although there may have been more notable moments, more historic moments, even more significant moments in St. Louis sports history, nothing moves the needle on the singular drama meter quite like that grand October night in Houston.

The date: October 17, 2005.

It was a cool Monday night in Minute Maid Park, and the retractable roof of the ballpark was sealed tighter than a drum. It was Game 5 of the NL championship series between the Cardinals and Houston Astros, with the Astros on the verge of victory and a trip to the World Series, holding a 3–1 edge in the best-of-seven series. Until this incredible moment, Minute Maid Park had been as noisy as a jet engine. But now, the hermetically sealed baseball amusement park was as quiet as a tomb. The only sound you could hear in the place was the shocking thunder of a ball being smashed by hard lumber. The only sight that mattered was this massive moon shot on a fast and furious trajectory toward the big glass windows beyond the train tracks 450 feet away from home plate.

"Ohhh ... MY ... GOSH!"

Those were the words everyone saw coming out of the gasping mouth of Houston starter Andy Pettitte as he stood in the dugout watching Cardinals slugger Albert Pujols blast one of the most dramatic home runs in baseball history.

In the ninth inning, the Redbirds—trailing 4–2—were on the verge of being eliminated from the NLCS. Now the ball was rocketing out toward the glass windows, and the Cardinals were going home with a stunning 5–4 victory. Although two nights later the Astros eliminated St. Louis and headed off to the World Series, on this wondrous night Pujols stole the show and silenced the crowd.

"It was so quiet in there I could actually hear the dirt underneath my cleats as I was running around the bases," Pujols would say.

If you could scan the crowd at the end of this stunning and improbable night, the only thing you would see was shock and awe: shock at the sudden-death end to their all-too-premature World Series celebrations, and awe at the magnificent, wrecking-crew power of one of the most impressive young hitters in major league history.

In dramatic fashion, Pujols was responsible for perhaps the most theatrical blast in the glorious postseason history of Cardinals baseball. This clout had the magnitude of a Reggie Jackson moment. It was as dramatic as Kirk Gibson's stiff-legged trot around the Dodger Stadium basepath. This was Bobby Thomson chilling. This was Carlton Fisk amazing. This was Bill Mazeroski magnificent.

With two runners on base and one out in the ninth, Brad Lidge, the Houston closer who had been the biggest thorn in the Cardinals' side, went from invincible reliever to historic goat—and perhaps permanently damaged as an effective closer—when he hung a 0–1 slider toward the plate against Pujols.

The ball jumped off Pujols's bat with raw urgency.

As soon as he made contact, Pujols did that grim-faced, matter-of-fact lip bite, then flipped his bat to the side with an arrogant disdain as this powerful blast rose high in the air. The home run ball split the pale green girders high above the left center field wall, crashed into the glass windows overlooking Crawford Street and the railroad tracks just below the CITGO sign, then ricocheted back onto the field.

With one breathless swing, Pujols ruined a delirious Minute Maid Park house party and officially gave birth to his burgeoning legend status.

As a result, Brad Lidge was never the same. The man who was once the most feared stopper in baseball lost his mojo that night. Two years later, his manager, Phil Garner, removed him from the closer role after too many late-inning failures.

59

WHAT WAS THE MOST DRAMATIC MOMENT IN CLASSIC ST. LOUIS BASEBALL HISTORY?

11 This argument is for the older-generation St. Louis sports fan. If the kids have Pujols and his bat, then the "Mad Dash" is the quintessential unforgettable moment for the more mature set. It was Game 7 of the 1946 World Series between the Cardinals and the Boston Red Sox, with the score tied at 3–3 in the bottom of the eighth inning. Future Hall of Fame outfielder Enos ("Country") Slaughter led off with a single, then stayed stuck on first after the next two batters failed to get a hit. With Harry Walker at the plate, Slaughter took off from first on a steal attempt just as Walker swung at the pitch.

Walker smoked one into the gap in center field. When Boston outfielder Leon Culberson threw the ball back into the infield, shortstop Johnny Pesky retrieved the throw, but hesitated for a split second.

That was all the time Slaughter needed. He ignored the stop sign from third base coach Mike Gonzalez and charged furiously down the third-base line. Seconds later, Slaughter was kicking up a cloud of white chalk as he slid across home plate safely for the game-winning run and a slice of baseball immortality. In 2003, *Time* magazine called it one of the 10 Greatest Moments in World Series history.

WHAT WAS THE MOST DRAMATIC MOMENT IN ST. LOUIS FOOTBALL HISTORY?

12 It was the best and most important tackle in St. Louis football history. Mike Jones, former University of Missouri running back turned NFL linebacker, wrapped his arms around Tennessee Titans wide receiver Kevin Dyson and wouldn't let him go.

In the closing seconds of the Rams' 23–16 Super Bowl XXXIV victory, Dyson was a few precious feet away from the Rams' end zone. Now he was stretched out with the football in his hand, reaching for the goal line with everyone in the Georgia Dome—and millions more watching on television—collectively holding their breath.

As he fell toward the ground in this agonizing slow-motion dream, it felt like you were watching a felled tree crashing to the ground, unsure whether it would slam into your house or fall harmlessly a few feet shy.

So sometimes, the football gods really do get it right.

Sometimes they conspire to put two equally matched teams on the field together on the game's biggest stage, allow them to trade blows for three delirious hours, then force you to hold onto your hearts for the final few seconds, not sure whether you should be whooping it up or begging for CPR.

Super Bowl XXXIV provided the most thrilling, heart-palpitating finish you ever saw in the NFL's championship game.

The Rams jumped out to a 16–0 third-quarter lead, only to see Tennessee tie it with 2 minutes 12 seconds remaining. Then Super Bowl MVP quarterback Kurt Warner, who threw for a Super Bowl record 414 yards, hooked up with wide receiver Isaac Bruce for a 73-yard touchdown with 1:54 left to push the Rams back on top at 23–16.

Now it was up to the Titans and quarterback Steve McNair to force overtime. McNair skillfully marched the Titans from their 12-yard line to first-and-goal at the Rams 10 with six seconds left.

The Georgia Dome felt like it was about to explode, there was so much nervous energy in the place. There was time for only one more play, and in the Tennessee huddle McNair called for a pass that was originally designed to go to the tight end. But at the last second he saw wide receiver Kevin

Dyson open on a slant pattern. Dyson caught the ball inside the 5-yard line and tried to curl into the end zone.

Now the world was in suspended animation. It whirled to a slo-mo crawl… that … left everyone… wondering….

Would he?

Could he?

Oh my gawd…

Dyson zeroed in on the ball, caught it, spun around, and saw… the end zone, and it was… right…*there…*

"As soon as I caught the ball, I was thinking 'paydirt,'" Dyson told reporters after the game. "I didn't think anybody would be in the middle of the field."

But Mike Jones was there, and he held on tight, wouldn't let go, couldn't let go. And Dyson fell to the ground inches shy of the end zone as the stadium clock ticked off the last seconds and the Rams went from potential heart attack victims to champions of the world. "The Tackle" became a freeze-frame moment that lingers forever in the hearts and minds of St. Louis sports lovers.

WHAT WAS THE MOST DRAMATIC MOMENT IN ST. LOUIS HOCKEY HISTORY?

13 The history of the Blues has been peppered with several dramatic overtime moments, like the uncanny comeback on November 29, 2000, when the Blues rallied from a 5–0 third-period deficit to beat the Toronto Maple Leafs 6–5 in overtime.

So how can a game that tied the largest comeback in NHL history not be considered the greatest in Blues history? As good as that game was, it had a few very important aspects that knocked it off the "greatest ever" pedestal. First of all, it was just a regular-season game. There was no championship hardware at stake, just a few valuable points in the regular-season standings.

Besides, how can this game be considered the "greatest" when no one ever gave it a nickname? Try as I could, no matter how much research I gathered looking back on the game, no reporter, columnist, or clever headline writer ever dubbed this game against the Leafs with a memorable moniker that would forever label it as something special.

So that left us with only one choice.

In the span of one historic hockey game, the St. Louis Blues managed to have their worst and finest hours. On May 12, 1986, in Game 6 of the Stanley Cup's Western Conference finals, a game forever known as "The Monday Night Miracle," the Blues were on the verge of elimination. But a three-goal blitz in the final 12 minutes of regulation, followed by a Doug Wickenheiser game-winner at 7:30 of overtime, produced the most significant comeback in Blues history in a 6–5 victory over the Calgary Flames.

With 12 minutes to go in the third period—and losing the best-of-seven series three games to two—St. Louis trailed the Flames, 5–2, when the "miracle" began to unfold. The Brian Sutter-Doug Gilmour-Greg Paslawski line kept the Blues alive by scoring three times in the last 12 minutes of regulation.

Sutter, who had been held without a goal for the entire playoffs, finally got one to pull St. Louis within 5–3. Then Paslawski scored twice in the last 4:11, with Sutter contributing an assist from the corner on the first goal. Paslawski would tie the game single-handedly with 1:08 to play, stealing the puck and firing a wicked shot in past Calgary's rookie goalie Jamie McCoun. With the home crowd at The Arena going mad, the game went into overtime, and suddenly the Blues felt like there was hope. That hope came to fruition at 7:30 of the overtime, when Doug Wickenheiser shoved the mortician aside with his second, game-winning goal.

65

The game stands on its own. However, after the delirium of Monday night, the season came to a heartbreaking end two nights later in Calgary as the Blues lost a lifeless 2–1 decision in Game 7 to miss out on the Stanley Cup finals for the fourth time since arriving in St. Louis.

THE TEAM'S
THE THING

THE BEST PRO TEAMS IN ST. LOUIS HISTORY

Once again, the rich history of St. Louis sports made this task a bit tricky. How do you select what is greatest? Must it be a championship team (oops, that would eliminate the Blues from this whole section), or does a great one that just fell short qualify? The Cardinals obviously have lots of winning options to choose from, and the Rams and long-gone Hawks had singular world championship seasons. Let's take a look at how they all stack up.

WHAT WAS THE GREATEST TEAM IN ST. LOUIS BASEBALL HISTORY:

The "Swifties," the "Gas House Gang," or the "El Birdos"?

14 Picking the best Cardinals team is a lot like choosing your favorite scoop of ice cream at Oberweis. It's a tough task, but with so many delicious dishes to choose from, ultimately you can never go wrong.

The longer I searched, the more difficult the task became. At first I thought there were only two teams to choose between: the "Gas House Gang" of the 1930s or the "Swifties" of the 1940s.

But the longer I looked, and the more people I talked to, it was important to add one more contemporary team to the mix—the 1967 world champions that everyone dubbed the "El Birdos." The 1967 Cardinals won 101 games and a World Series with five future Hall of Famers in uniform: pitchers Bob Gibson and Steve Carlton, plus Lou Brock and Orlando Cepeda and manager Red Schoendienst. We'll talk more about them later.

The "Gas House Gang" was the Cardinals team best known as a rowdy collection of players with colorful nicknames that perfectly fit their eccentric personalities. With "Pepper" Martin, Dizzy and Daffy Dean, Leo Durocher, Pat Crawford, and Frankie Frisch, the Redbirds won three NL pennants (1930, 1931, and 1934) and two World Series (1931 and 1934).

The 1930 National League champs had a team batting average of .314, with every Cardinals player's regular batting average over .300, led by right fielder George Watkins who hit a team rookie record .373.

However, the club won 100 games only once in the decade, and between the two World Series crowns dropped to a sixth-place 72–82 record in 1932 and a fifth-place 82–71 mark the following year.

69

Meanwhile, the Cardinals of the early 1940s, known as the "Swifties," did not have any drop-off during their run of NL domination.

Specifically, the 1942 "Swifties" that won 106 games—a franchise record—are regarded in most knowledgeable baseball circles as among the greatest baseball teams of all time.

The 1942 "Swifties" needed only five games to beat the New York Yankees in the World Series, then came back over the next two seasons to win a whopping 210 regular-season games and make more trips to the World Series, losing to the Yankees in 1943 before coming back to beat the crosstown St. Louis Browns in 1944.

Let's savor those numbers for one more moment so that you understand just how dominant this team was:

- 316 victories over three seasons, which is an average of over 105 wins per season.
- 3 consecutive trips to the World Series.
- 2 World Series championships in three years.

But it only gets better. By 1946, the Cardinals were back in the World Series again and beat the Boston Red Sox in a thrilling seven-game series. From 1942 to 1946, the greatest stretch of domination in franchise history, the team won four NL pennants in five years and three world championships.

However, it's still not enough to get the nod here. The

most intriguing team in Cardinals history is that positively loaded "El Birdos" team.

How do you pick against a team that won 100 games in three consecutive seasons, and won 316 out of 462 games like the "Swifties" did between 1942–44?

It's not easy, but let me do a bit of qualification. Many will argue that the best years of the "Swifties" domination occurred during the early 1940s when major league baseball's talent pool was diminished by World War II, and I can't disagree.

But it is impressive nonetheless that the Cards did dominate as much as they did when the team's two Hall of Famers—Stan Musial and Enos Slaughter—both missed a combined four seasons between 1943–45 (Musial in 1945 and Slaughter in 1943 through 1945) due to military service.

Still, when picking between a great team post-1947 or a great team pre-1947, I'll go with the post-integration team every time. With the early 1940s National League watered-down because of both the war and the lack of black players in the majors, pro baseball just wasn't as strong during the early 1940s as it was at the height of the mid- to late-1960s.

Furthermore, the 1967 Cardinals team was amazing, a genuine melting pot of talent. Not only was this a team filled with great black and white players, it was one of the first Cardinals teams to field Latin players. The 1967 team also had another unique distinction. It had the first million-dollar

71

payroll in sports history. Remember the famous *Sports Illustrated* cover photo with the Cards players in street clothes sitting in front of their locker stalls? No team had ever assembled such an expensive—at least by the times—roster. And the Cardinals clearly got their money's worth, because the mid-1960s Redbirds went to the World Series three times between 1964 and 1968, winning two world championships in memorable seven-game series with the New York Yankees and Boston Red Sox and losing a seven-game series in 1968 to the Detroit Tigers.

Gibson was particularly dominant that year before missing 52 games when a line drive off the bat of Pittsburgh's Roberto Clemente broke Gibson's right leg. But he returned in time for the postseason, winning three games in the World Series with a 1.00 ERA. In that series, Gibby pitched all three complete games, gave up 14 hits, only allowed three runs, and struck out 26 batters while surrendering just five walks. Meanwhile, Brock became the first player in baseball history to hit 20 home runs and steal 50 bases in a season (21 dingers, 52 stolen bases) and batted .299 in the regular season. In the World Series, he batted .414 as the leadoff man, scoring eight runs, collecting 12 hits, stealing seven bases, and maintaining an on-base percentage of .452.

Cepeda joined the Cardinals in 1967, and his signing paid off immediately with a .325 batting average, 25 homers, and a league-leading 111 RBI on his way to winning the NL MVP. This stockpiled team also included Mike Shannon, Roger Maris, and 14-game winners Steve Carlton and Nelson Briles, plus Dick Hughes, who was 16-6.

The "El Birdos" were the best team in franchise history. They weren't paid a million bucks for nothing.

WHAT WAS THE GREATEST TEAM IN ST. LOUIS FOOTBALL HISTORY:

The 1999 Greatest Show on Turf or the Greatest Show on Turf Version 2.1?

Let's not waste much time including the football Cardinals in this conversation. Sorry, but in order to merit inclusion in this debate, you need to have at least sniffed the Super Bowl.

So that leaves us with only Dick Vermeil's Super Bowl champion Rams from 1999 and Mike Martz's 2001 Super Bowl runner-ups. It's too obvious to say the 1999 Rams win simply because they won Super Bowl XXXIV, because a whole lot of folks in St. Louis still believe that the 2001

Rams *should have* won Super Bowl XXXVI (more on that in Argument 53).

So let's break it down statistically. Here's a comparison of the two teams' offensive statistics:

	1999 Rams	**2001 Rams**
Record:	13–3	14–2
Av. yards/game:	400.8	418.1
Av. pass/game:	272.1	291.4
Av. rush/game:	272.1	126.7
Points scored:	526	503

Now the defenses:

	1999 Rams	**2001 Rams**
Av. yards/game:	293.6	279.4
Av. pass/game:	219.3	193.6
Av. rush/game:	74.3	85.9
Points allowed:	242	273

So far, the stats make it a push. The 2001 Rams offense produced more yards, but the 1999 Rams produced more points. The 2001 Rams gave up fewer yards, but the 1999 Rams allowed fewer points. So we have to delve a bit deeper.

On the 1999 team, Kurt Warner had one of the greatest seasons by a quarterback in NFL history, throwing for 41 touchdowns, 4,353 yards, and earning a staggering 109.2 quarterback rating. Marshall Faulk was equally brilliant, with more than 1,000 yards rushing (1,381) and receiving (1,048). Add in Isaac Bruce's 77 catches for 1,165 yards and 12 touchdowns, kicker Jeff Wilkins's 124 points, and the return men Joe Horne (29.7 yard kick return average and two touchdowns) and Az-Zahir Hakim (10.5 yard punt return average, 1 touchdown), and it's easy to see how explosive the world champion Rams were.

But in 2001, Warner was the NFL's MVP. He threw for almost 500 more yards, completed 50 more passes, and had a stunning 68.1 completion percentage, along with 36 touchdowns to boot. Faulk, who finished second in the MVP voting, was even more dangerous, scoring a staggering 21 touchdowns and 128 points. He even went over 200 yards rushing in a regular-season game versus Carolina, and averaged 105 yards rushing in three playoff games. The 2001 team also had a fully developed Torry Holt on the roster, which gave the Rams a rare treat of two 1,000-yard wide receivers (Holt had 81 catches, 1,363 yards, 7 touchdowns; Bruce had 64 catches, 1,106 yards, 6 touchdowns).

So here's the answer: The 2001 Rams *should have been* the best team in St. Louis pro football history. If they had completed the job in Super Bowl XXXVI against the New England Patriots (and if Mike Martz had given the ball more to Faulk— again, more on that later), there would have been no debate in my mind that these Rams were slightly superior to the 1999 Rams. But finishing the job needs to account for something, and that's why Vermeil's Rams edge out Martz's Rams.

WHAT WAS THE GREATEST TEAM IN ST. LOUIS BASKETBALL HISTORY:

The 1958 Hawks or the 1968 Hawks?

16 Believe it or not, the Boston Celtics were not the only dominant team in the National Basketball Association during the late 1950s and early 1960s. The St. Louis Hawks were right there playing the perfect foil.

The Hawks reached the NBA finals four consecutive times between 1957 and 1961, captured four Western Conference titles in that period, and also rolled to six division titles, 10 conference titles, and 12 playoff appearances in their brief 13 seasons in St. Louis. And while the Celtics were clearly the NBA's elite team in that era, in order to win all those NBA titles Boston often had to go through the Hawks on their way to building a dynasty.

In other words, there's a quality selection of teams to choose from in adding to the list of St. Louis' greatest sports teams. We ultimately narrowed the choices down to the two most worthy teams, the 1957–58 Hawks and St. Louis' final NBA team, the 1967–68 Hawks.

The last St. Louis Hawks team was, at least on paper, the best basketball team this city ever saw. That 1968 squad won its first seven games of the season, got off to a 16–1 start, and reeled off a franchise-best 56–26 record for the Hawks' sixth and final division title before leaving for Atlanta.

Future Hall of Famer Lenny Wilkens (20 point average, 8.3 assists, 5.3 rebounds) was the point guard, and another future Hall of Fame inductee, Paul Silas (13.4 points, 11.7 rebounds), was banging the boards at power forward. Zelmo Beaty (21.1 points, 11.7 rebounds), Bill Bridges (15.6 points, 13.4 rebounds), Don Ohl (13.1 points), and "Sweet" Lou Hudson (12.5 points) joined this high-scoring (113 points a game) squad that blitzed through the NBA's Western Division.

But as impressive as the regular season was (the Hawks won the Western Division by four games over the Los Angeles Lakers), the postseason was a huge disappointment. Going against the third-place San Francisco Warriors, who finished a full 13 games behind the Hawks in the regular season, the Hawks lost Game 2 at home and went on the road only to fall behind in the best-of-seven series 3 games to 1, before being eliminated in the sixth game.

The 1957–58 Hawks did not have quite as regular-season success as the 1967–68 squad, but the 41–31 record was still good enough to win the Western Division regular season. In the postseason, the Hawks had an easy path into the NBA finals. In the old, eight-team league, the winners of the Eastern (Boston Celtics) and Western (Hawks) Divisions had first-round playoff byes. So the Hawks faced a Detroit Pistons team in the Conference finals that won only 33 games in the regular season, and easily beat them four games to one.

What this decision comes down to is very simple. The 1957–58 Hawks won the franchise's only NBA title (four games to three) by knocking off a Celtics team that included six future Hall of Famers (Bill Russell, Bob Cousy, K.C. Jones, Bill Sharman, Tom Heinsohn, and Frank Ramsey). That 1957–58 St. Louis squad wasn't too shabby either, with four future Hall of Famers in Bob Pettit, Ed Macauley, Slater Martin, and Cliff Hagan. The series went to seven games, and in one of the most memorable finals performances in NBA history, Pettit was practically unstoppable, scoring 50 points in a 110–108 victory. Advantage: 1958 Hawks.

WHAT WAS THE GREATEST TEAM IN ST. LOUIS HOCKEY HISTORY:

The 1981 Blues or the 2000 Blues?

17 Picking the best all-time Blues team is not without its challenges. Unlike all the other professional franchises in St. Louis, the Blues have spent 40 years in the city without a championship, which makes choosing the all-time greatest hockey team just a bit problematic.

What we're left to choose from are an assortment of high caliber regular-season teams that are stained by the disappointment of postseason failure. Twenty-five consecutive trips to the postseason without a Stanley Cup title gives us plenty to work with, doesn't it? After sorting through the history books, it comes down to two obvious choices: the 1980–81 Blues and the 1999–2000 Blues, two teams that best symbolize the excitement and disappointment this franchise has annually produced.

The 1980–81 Blues (45–18–17) finished the regular season with a then-team record 107 points and a first-place finish in the Smythe Division. They were the surprise team of the NHL, as they were only two years removed from a disastrous 18-win season (48 points). The 1980–81 Blues were the second-best team in the league, with a potent scoring lineup that included a fresh set of stars like Wayne Babych (54 goals), future Hall of Famer Bernie Federko, Brian Sutter, outstanding goalie Mike Liut, and a roster that included 10 players with 20 or more goals.

Of course, like every team in franchise history, the 1980–81 Blues will be most noted for their shocking exit in the playoffs, when they were ousted from the second round by the 13th-place New York Rangers.

That leaves us with the 1999–2000 Blues, who won a franchise record 51 games, clinched the Central Division, and captured the NHL's President's Trophy by finishing the regular season with a league-high (and franchise record) 114 points. Of course, the playoffs rolled around and the Blues were ousted after one round by another inferior team.

So how do we decide between two disappointing teams?

Maybe the best measuring stick is the degree of disappointment. The 2000 team probably was the greatest downer, because no one saw this one coming. This team sent five players to the NHL All-Star Game, won a franchise record number of games, had the best regular-season record in the league, and was heavily regarded as the most likely team to break the franchise's postseason frustrations.

Maybe we all should have known better, but we didn't. In hindsight it's easy to see that they weren't big enough up front, with small skill players Pierre Turgeon, Pavol

Demitra, Lubos Baretcko, Marty Reasoner, Scott Young, and Ladislav Nagy just too undersized to handle the rough tactics that the San Jose Sharks employed in the Western Conference quarterfinals.

In the regular season, the Blues were able to overcome that lack of size with speed and standout goaltending. But in the playoffs, with the referees calling a different—and decidedly tolerant—game, the Blues could not flourish.

In the playoffs, goalie Roman Turek saw all his stats fall off dramatically. He posted a 1.95 goals-against average with a .912 save percentage in the regular season, but in the playoffs those numbers changed drastically (2.75 GAA and a .822 save percentage).

When you look at all the numbers, and calculate the two disappointments, the 2000 team was the greater letdown and left the city's hockey faithful with the biggest hangover.

That means the 1980–81 Blues gain the slightest edge as the best hockey team in St. Louis history.

HOW SWEET (AND AWFUL) IT IS

THE BEST TRADES IN ST. LOUIS HISTORY

This was a hard one, since the men who have been running St. Louis sports franchises over the years have been fairly smart guys. The good trades made over the years have far outweighed the really bad ones.

Determining which trades belonged on the list was a rather uncomplicated process. How good were the players when they were traded? If an over-the-hill St. Louis player was dispatched to the hinterlands, that doesn't weigh quite as heavily as sending off a player seemingly in his prime. We broke it up into sports; and of course, because of its long history in town, baseball dominated the discussion.

WHAT WAS THE BEST TRADE IN ST. LOUIS BASEBALL HISTORY?

18   3. MARK McGWIRE FROM THE OAKLAND A's TO THE CARDINALS FOR RELIEVER T. J. MATHEWS AND MINOR LEAGUE PITCHERS ERIC LUDWICK AND BLAKE STEIN.

Big Mac became a legend in St. Louis (albeit a chemically enhanced one), banging record numbers of home runs over the fence. He broke Roger Maris's single-season home run record, finished with more than 500 career homers, and was well on his way to the Hall of Fame before drug suspicions ruined—or at least stalled—his Cooperstown admission.

As it turns out, the Cardinals got the better of this trade both short and long term, because while McGwire became a baseball legend in St. Louis, none of the pitchers the Cards sent to Oakland turned into stars. Ludwick finished his four-year major league career with a 2–10 record, Stein finished a five-year major league career with a 21–28 record and two career saves, while Mathews finished his eight-year career with a 32–26 record and 16 saves.

2. WILLIE McGEE FROM THE YANKEES TO THE CARDINALS FOR PITCHER BOB SYKES.

This one was actually more lopsided than our winner. The Yankees sent their former first-round draft pick McGee to the Cards for a pitcher who would never play another game in the majors. Meanwhile, all McGee did was become an NL MVP, lead the league in batting twice, and take the Cards to a 1982 World Series victory with his stellar play at the plate (two homers in Game 3) and brilliant glove work.

McGee became one of the most popular players in the history of the franchise, and was a key member of Whitey Herzog's fast and furious teams of the 1980s.

1. LOU BROCK FROM THE CHICAGO CUBS TO THE CARDINALS FOR PITCHER ERNIE BROGLIO.

Can there be any other deal that ranks higher than the one hailed roundly in St. Louis and cursed forever in Chicago?

The Brock for Broglio trade is widely regarded as one of the most lopsided deals in major league baseball history, and with good reason. On June 15, 1964, the Cards sent pitcher Ernie Broglio, Bobby Shantz, and Doug Clemens to the Cubs for Brock and pitchers Jack Spring and Paul Toth.

The other guys aren't that important in this one. This deal was all about Brock and Broglio. Let's begin with understanding why the Cubs were so tempted. Broglio was coming off an 18–8 season. Two years earlier he was 21–9.

He had 38 complete games in the four seasons leading up to the trade and had a career ERA of roughly 3.00. Yet as soon as he came to the Cubs, he pitched like . . . well, like he was with the Cubs. He had only 33 more career starts, a 7–19 record, and was out of baseball two years later due to a sore arm that many Northsiders still believe the Cardinals knew about and kept secret.

With the Cubs, Lou Brock was just a decent player. His career batting average in his first three years in the majors was a little over .260, and he had only 50 stolen bases in 2½ seasons. And the Cubs organization didn't think very highly of him in right field, either.

But the Cardinals saw his promise, and in the 100 remaining games in that 1964 season, he batted .348 and helped the Cards leap from eighth place in the National League all the way to a World Series victory over the New York Yankees. By the end of his career, Brock was considered the greatest base-stealer of all time, had a career batting average of .293, led the National League in steals eight times, had 12 seasons with 50 or more stolen bases, set the major league record for most steals in a season (118), finished with 3,023 hits, and was inducted into the Hall of Fame.

Brock, a six-time All-Star, also played in three World Series and had a career World Series batting average of a stunning .391 in 21 games.

WHAT WAS THE BEST TRADE IN ST. LOUIS HOCKEY HISTORY?

19 When the Blues traded Rob Ramage and goalie Rick Wamsley to the Calgary Flames for Brett Hull on March 7, 1988, it turned out to be the most significant move in the history of the franchise. What the Blues got was the most popular and productive player in team history.

In his first season, Brett Hull scored 41 goals and captured the Lady Byng Memorial Trophy, given to honor a player for great sportsmanship and gentlemanly conduct. Two years later, he went on a scoring roll, putting together three consecutive 70-plus goal seasons, which included a career high 86 goals in 1990–91, earning him the Lester B. Pearson Trophy and the Hart Memorial Trophy as the league's MVP.

Hull spent 11 seasons in St. Louis, breaking the Blues all-time record for goals in a season with 72 in 1989–90. The following season, when Hull shattered his own mark by scoring 86 goals, he scored 50 goals in 49 games, becoming the first Blues player to score 50 goals in 50 games or less. In 1991–92, he became the second player in NHL history to score 50 goals in 50 games twice. He still holds the all-time Blues franchise record in goals (527), hat tricks (27), game-winning goals (70), power play goals (195), and shots on goal (3,367), and ranks second in assists (409), points (936), and shorthanded goals (18).

In contrast, Ramage was a bit player on the Flames' 1989 Stanley Cup championship team, and bounced around the league until 1994. Wamsley played five more seasons with the Flames and Toronto Maple Leafs as a backup goalie.

WHAT WAS THE BEST TRADE IN ST. LOUIS FOOTBALL HISTORY?

20 Football is a sport that tends to shy away from trading superstars. Most of the moves tend to come on or around the NFL draft, and they usually involve swapping picks, not established superstar players. Trading draft picks for draft picks is a less risky proposition and easier to engineer in the conservative NFL. So while the clever 1997 draft-day trade with the New York Jets that landed the Rams the first pick in the draft and future Pro Bowl offensive tackle Orlando Pace was a good one, it was not the best.

The Jets were not giving away a proven star. They were not handing over a sure-fire multidimensional Pro Bowler.

So the Rams get more props for the move that allowed them to complete a 1999 pre-draft trade that landed them Indianapolis Colts Pro Bowl running back Marshall Faulk, who became the final piece to a Super Bowl puzzle.

Traded on April 15, 1999, for the Rams' second-round (36th overall) and fifth-round (138th overall) picks, the Rams couldn't have imagined how well—and totally lopsided—this deal would be for them. They acquired a man who would become, for a three- or four-year period, the most dangerous all-around running back in pro football. With Mike Martz creating an offense that would highlight every bit of Faulk's athletic excellence, No. 28 would lead the Rams to two Super Bowls and cement his legend as an almost certain future NFL Hall of Fame player. And all they had to give up were two draft picks that the Colts used to select linebacker Mike Peterson out of Florida and Brad Scioli, a defensive end from Penn State.

Who?

Yeah, exactly. The fact that you need to ask who these two players are further highlights how big a coup this was for the Rams. Scioli played six NFL seasons in Indianapolis, logging 121 tackles and 15 sacks in 80 games before retiring in 2005 at age 28 with aggravated pain from an arthritic shoulder. He was the ultimate JAG ("Just A Guy"), who played in the league yet never left a lasting footprint.

Peterson was a bit more successful (he's still in the NFL), having played eight seasons with the Colts and Jacksonville Jaguars. The Colts had him for four years. During that time he collected 4 ½ sacks, and he developed into a reliable starting middle linebacker for both the Colts and Jags. But no one will ever look back on this trade and say anything other than the Rams won this one hands down.

THE WORST TRADES IN ST. LOUIS HISTORY

We already told you about a trade of historic badness earlier in the book. It's arguably the worst decision—albeit an understandable one—in sports history: St. Louis Hawks owner Ben Kerner gave away the draft rights to Bill Russell to the Boston Celtics for Ed Macauley and Cliff Hagan. The trade made sense at the time on a couple of levels. First, Macauley had family issues with an ill son who needed constant medical treatment, so "Easy Ed" wanted to return home to St. Louis. Second, as a businessman, Kerner probably knew that the best way to box-office success in a racially charged city like St. Louis in the 1950s was to continue fielding teams that relied heavily on white stars, not black ones.

So he probably felt forced into making the deal that would send away one of the greatest players in NBA history, a player who would have likely guaranteed him a long run of championships. Even though Hagan and "Easy Ed" would help the Hawks to the 1958 NBA championship and four trips to the NBA finals in six years, Russell would lead Boston to a dynasty that

90

would win 10 titles over the next 11 seasons. Just from a historic point of view, it's hard to top that transaction, which is why it deserved to be the worst moment in St. Louis sports history. Who knows: If Russell (and former Hawks head coach Red Auerbach) had come to St. Louis instead of Boston, think how much different the pro basketball landscape could have been.

Would the Hawks still be in St. Louis? Would this have become a long-standing NBA town like Chicago, Milwaukee, or Detroit, or would the racial dynamics of the place have made it almost impossible not to become a failed NBA city and a burgeoning NHL town? Would the Hawks have turned into a dynasty with Russell leading the way, or would Kerner have still abandoned the city in 1968 for Atlanta?

It sure does make you wonder, doesn't it?

So with the Hawks' bungling move already relegated to a more elevated plateau on the dark side of sports infamy in St. Louis, we are left with the following entries to ponder as the worst trades in the history of this town.

WHAT WAS THE WORST TRADE IN ST. LOUIS BASEBALL HISTORY?

21 Poor Rick Wise was a decent pitcher for the Philadelphia Phillies, arriving in the majors at 18 years old in 1964. By 1971, he was the best pitcher on a bad last-place team, winning 17 games with an impressive 2.88 ERA. He even threw a no-hitter against the Cincinnati Reds.

But he will always be known as the guy on the wrong end of the worst trade in Cardinals history, the 1972 trade of star pitcher Steve Carlton.

Auggie Busch, the venerable owner of the Cards, was so angry about a contract dispute with his star left-hander that he foolishly made it public that he wanted Carlton gone. Carlton had earned $55,000 in 1971, his break-through sixth season in the majors, when he went 20–9. He wanted a $10,000 raise, and Busch wouldn't give it to him. In spring training, Busch petulantly decided to get rid of the kid and let everyone know it.

That was a huge mistake on many fronts.

The minute word of Busch's wishes spread throughout the baseball world, there wasn't a general manager who wasn't prepared to play hardball with the Redbirds.

As a result, the best offer they could get for Carlton was Wise, who would go 32–28 over his two-year stint with the Cardinals. Meanwhile, Carlton won 27 games for the last-place Phillies in 1972, and went on to a dominating Hall of Fame career with 329 victories, helping the Phillies to two World Series trips and six postseason visits in 14 years in Philadelphia.

And the Cardinals let him go over $10,000, one of the worst ideas to ever come out of the brewery.

Here's a footnote to this argument: Over the next few years, we may look back on the 2004 trade that brought All-Star pitcher Mark Mulder here from Oakland in the same light as the Carlton trade. Mulder had his moments, but spent much of the 2006 and 2007 seasons on the disabled list. Meanwhile, the A's received talented youngsters like pitcher Danny Haren, who has turned into one of the most promising young pitchers in baseball, and Daric Barton, who is developing into a top minor-league hitting prospect. Give this one a few more years before pronouncing a verdict.

WHAT WAS THE WORST TRADE IN ST. LOUIS HOCKEY HISTORY?

Why not nominate the August 4, 1995, trade in which the Blues traded goalie Curtis Joseph and right winger Mike Grier to Edmonton for first-round picks in 1996 and 1997? This draft-day miscue belongs in the conversation for sure. CuJo was a goalie on the rise, whose win totals increased in each of his first five seasons, and he was a fan favorite. But General Manager/Coach Mike Keenan had signed a declining Grant Fuhr in the 1995 off-season, and he made up his mind that the veteran Fuhr, not the kid CuJo, was his man.

So CuJo and another young prospect, Grier, were packaged to the Oilers. Why is this such a bad trade? Well, the two first-round picks the Blues got for Joseph and Grier were *their* picks—the Blues had previously relinquished them to Edmonton when Keenan signed Shayne Corson.

One other trade stands out as a truly bad deal by the Blues: the 2005 trade that sent Blues All-Star Chris Pronger to Edmonton for defensemen Eric Brewer, Doug Lynch, and Jeff Woywitka. This was one of those trades that set the franchise back for the foreseeable future and left disgruntled

Blues fans convinced that owner Bill Laurie was stripping the franchise down to a non-competitive mess. Under the old ownership that was trying to make the team more attractive for sale, the Blues basically gave their All-Star defenseman away for next to nothing.

Funny how what goes around comes around. When Pronger arrived in St. Louis, the fans hated him because he was replacing the very popular Brendan Shanahan. This time, they were angry at management for trading away a man who had turned into one of the Blues' best and most popular players.

Yet as bad as the Pronger deal was (he ended up winning two Stanley Cup titles after leaving St. Louis), nothing touches our winner: the Blues trading forward Craig Johnson, defenseman Roman Vopat, forward Patrice Tardif, and the No. 1 and No. 5 picks to the Los Angeles Kings for Wayne Gretzky. When the deal was originally made with 18 games left in the 1995–96 season, it was a great deal for the Blues, and easily could have dropped into the Best Trades category. The long-term prospect of "The Great One" and Brett Hull playing together was intriguing to say the least.

But it didn't take long for the excitement of the trade to burn off. Keenan's abrasive manner had already alienated him from Hull, and Gretzky quickly discovered that Keenan was not someone he wanted to play for over a long period of time.

95

Keenan sabotaged any hope of keeping Gretzky because of the bad blood that built up over the course of the final two months of the season. Keenan's attitude so ticked off Gretzky that "The Great One" was gone as soon as he could be, signing a free-agent deal with the New York Rangers after the season and leaving the Blues empty-handed.

It's not quite as bad as Kerner trading away the rights to Bill Russell, but it's awfully close. How can you spend all that effort to bring in the world's greatest hockey player, then just as quickly make him think he'd rather play in traffic than skate on the same ice with your coach?

WHAT WAS THE WORST TRADE IN ST. LOUIS FOOTBALL HISTORY?

23 Try this one: The Rams trade Jerome Bettis to Pittsburgh for a second- and fourth-round pick.

After beginning his NFL career with two consecutive Pro Bowl seasons in Los Angeles, former first-round draft pick Jerome Bettis came to St. Louis in 1995 and struggled with injuries. After two 1,000-yard plus seasons, the former Notre Dame star's rushing yardage and carries declined dramatically in his first year in St. Louis. He gained only 637 yards and averaged a paltry 3.3 yards a carry. He also ran into a personality conflict with Rams management. So in the off-season the Rams engineered a trade with the Pittsburgh Steelers that sent Bettis to the Iron City for a second-round pick in the 1996 NFL draft and a fourth-round pick in 1997. How'd that work out? Well, Bettis went on to rank No. 5 on the NFL's all-time career rushing list, and he's a certain future Hall of Famer. Those two draft picks turned into tight end Ernie Conwell (second in 1996), a decent tight end for the Rams' championship teams, and the fourth-round pick was part of the four-pick package sent to the Jets in 1997 for the draft rights to No. 1 draft pick Orlando Pace.

Topping off this awful move was the notion that all-time knucklehead Lawrence Phillips (their first round pick in 1996) could replace Bettis.

Surprisingly, though, this was not the worst trade we ever saw in St. Louis football history. In 2001, the Rams made one good move and turned it into an awful mistake. The good move was trading quarterback Trent Green to the Kansas City Chiefs for the 12th pick in the first round of the 2001 NFL draft. This deal made loads of sense because Green was coming off an injury that had him replaced in the starting lineup by two-time NFL MVP Kurt Warner. The Rams, of course, failed to capitalize on the trade, because they used that draft pick to select defensive

97

tackle Damione Lewis, a huge bust who never provided the strong inside run-stuffing presence the team needed.

It was bad enough that Lewis never proved to be a reliable starter. But one pick later, the Jacksonville Jaguars selected defensive tackle Marcus Stroud, who became a Pro Bowl player and just the sort of run-stuffing beast the Rams are still looking for six years later. Stroud wasn't the only Pro Bowl talent the Rams passed up on with that 12th pick, because five slots later the Seattle Seahawks chose future Pro Bowl offensive lineman Steven Hutchinson.

TALKIN' BASEBALL

CARDINALS—CUBS:

Is It Really a "Great" Rivalry?

24 Try not to take this the wrong way, but the Cardinals versus the Chicago Cubs is not a great sports rivalry.

This is not an insult (at least not to the Cardinals). It's a compliment to the Redbirds' decidedly more important status on the baseball food chain and the Cubs' perpetual state of slapstick failure.

Ali–Frazier had muscle. The Celtics and Lakers were stylistic rivals who equally divided a basketball nation and constantly provided us with lovely hoop championship wars. Heck, even the Rams versus the San Francisco 49ers back in the day was more compelling than the Cards–Cubs.

A great rivalry needs history, not just geo-social hatred and civic envy. A great rivalry needs clashing styles and competitive substance. It needs one team historically denying another's rite of championship passage. The Chicago Bulls and the Detroit Pistons have a rivalry like that. The New York Yankees and Boston Red Sox have a legendary rivalry like that, too.

What the Cards and Cubs have evokes no such lasting championship images. This one pales in comparison to other great rivalries for one overriding reason:

They rarely play games of consequence.

The Yanks and Sox engage in passionate high-stakes baseball wars in which division titles and trips to the World Series always seem to be at stake. The Cards and Cubs never play for anything important: The Cubs are rarely in contention for anything and the Redbirds always are. Since Tony La Russa became manager in 1996, the Cardinals have finished in first place in the NL Central seven times in 11 years.

Just because the hopeless Cubs fans say it's a rivalry doesn't make it so. Just because they get all giddy when they sweep a series in April or May, or even win two out of three from the Cards in August, it's still no more a great rivalry between these two teams than the Cards vs. the Brewers.

I know how much Cardinals fans love to travel 300 miles to Wrigley Field to see the Redbirds play. But Cardinals fans go everywhere to see the Redbirds play, and proximity doesn't necessarily make for a great rivalry. After all, the Cards reside in the same state with the sorry, no-account Kansas City Royals, but we all know that the only people who regard Cards–Royals as a "rivalry" are the KC fans who have perpetual inferiority complexes against the "big city folks" in St. Louis.

Even though the Tony La Russa–Dusty Baker dugout dustups added some particularly entertaining spice to the battles of the early 2000s, it takes more than managers

101

cussing at each other from the top of their dugout steps to create a hot-blooded baseball conflict.

You cannot have a great rivalry just because you want it to be a great rivalry. You cannot have a great rivalry just because as fans you hate the other guys as much as they hate you. Cards–Cubs will become a meaningful baseball war the minute the Cubs are at least in the hunt for a World Series at the same time the Cardinals are.

Go to a Yanks–Sox game in either Boston or New York and you'll understand what a true great sports rivalry is. In April these games feel like October classics; there is that much energy in the ballpark.

In contrast, go to a Cards–Cubs game in August or September, and it's just a good excuse to have a cold beer.

WAS BOB GIBSON'S 1968 SEASON THE GREATEST PROFESSIONAL ACHIEVEMENT IN ST. LOUIS SPORTS HISTORY?

25 To me, the essence of greatness in sports is when your performance is so masterful that you alter the way your sport is played.

When your dominance of the competition is so complete and uncontrollable that the only answer is to change the rules to handicap your athletic supremacy, that's when you know you've climbed to an otherworldly plateau.

So when flipping through the history pages of St. Louis sports, you can certainly come up with an abundance of miracle moments of domination, whether it was a man batting over .400, a man hammering 70 home runs, or a football team becoming an almost unstoppable offensive show. Yet none of these shows of force resulted in the sport changing its rules to slow them down. Only one St. Louis athlete can lay that claim to fame: Bob Gibson.

Gibson's dominance during the 1968 season is unprecedented. His ungodly earned run average of 1.12 was one of the tipping points in major league baseball's decision to lower the height of the pitcher's mound from 15 inches to 10.

The belief was that Gibby and the other dominant pitchers of his era simply had way too much leverage firing strikes off that high profile mound. In 1968, the National League collective batting average was .243. In the American League it was only .230, with both leagues producing an average of roughly 3.42 runs a game.

In that season, Gibson struck out 268 batters and threw a league-leading 13 shutouts. During one 99-inning stretch, he surrendered a total of two runs. But we need to take a closer look at what Gibson accomplished to realize just how much more outrageous his season *could have* been.

The truth is, with just a little bit of help, Gibson could have had one of the most amazing seasons in baseball history.

The biggest number we will remember is the eye-popping earned run average, the lowest ERA in baseball history for any pitcher with 300 or more innings pitched. Yet despite the record-setting ERA, Gibson's won–loss record was only 22–9 in 1968. He was barely giving up 1 run a game in his 34 starts, and it's hard to understand how he could have actually lost nine games being so dominant.

Looking back on how he lost those nine games, what you're left with is how little run support he got. The Cardinals were actually shut out in three of those nine games, with San Francisco Giants Hall of Famer Gaylord

Perry no-hitting the Cards and another Hall of Famer, Dodger Don Drysdale, tossing the third of his record six consecutive shutouts against the Redbirds. In the other shutout loss, the only run that was scored came in the 10th inning of a complete game against Philadelphia. In another loss, Cubs Hall of Famer Ferguson Jenkins tossed a three-hitter in a 5–1 victory and gave up the only run with two outs in the ninth inning. In his nine losses, Gibson posted a 2.14 ERA, yet the Cards were outscored 27–12 in those games.

Gibson was so good in 1968 that, according to BaseballAnalysts.com, if the Cardinals had produced just four runs in each of Gibson's 34 starts, he would have gone a staggering 30–2. Yet to me the stat pearl that really jumps out is this one, also from BaseballAnalysts.com: If the Cards had only scored one lousy run in every game he pitched, Gibson still would have managed to finish the season with a 13–10 record.

That's just filthy, nasty, and unbelievably spectacular.

DOES MARK McGWIRE BELONG IN THE HALL OF FAME?

26 The answer is a big and simple "No."

In my opinion, Mark McGwire is a drug cheat whose greatest baseball moments were fueled by the tip of a steroid-filled syringe. And McGwire has no one to blame but himself for this rejection—which was confirmed in 2007.

Even while he stays in his self-imposed exile, McGwire remains an easy target for baseball's Hall of Fame voters. Stung by the memory of buying into his record-breaking season of 1998, the Hall whacked Big Mac's once-heroic reputation with a stunning vengeance as they denied him election to the Hall of Fame class of 2007.

McGwire—once considered a national hero, now a larger-than-life symbol of baseball's steroids era—was excluded by a staggering 76.5 percent of the electorate. Keeping Big Mac out of Cooperstown in his first year of eligibility goes under the category of "Dog bites man..." It wasn't exactly shocking news. It was precisely the right thing to do, striking down the first known (or widely suspected) drug cheat of the steroids era who became eligible for the Hall.

Yet it remains to be seen how long Big Mac will be on the outside of Cooperstown looking in. Was the overwhelming rejection by the Baseball Writers' Association a strong rebuke or a show of fleeting temperance? Will that 23.5 percent "yes" vote continue to increase in large percentages so rapidly that we'll soon look back at this year as a grandstanding farce?

I worry that some voters will now turn around and confirm his nomination after the first-year "not" vote, feeling that the 2007 rejection was a way to "make him pay." I know some voters are thinking this way. But I think that mentality is dumb and unproductive, because I don't recall ever seeing one Hall of Fame plaque inscribed with the notation, "Oh, this guy isn't a real Hall of Famer because he didn't get into Cooperstown until after the fifth year on the ballot." Last time I checked, there wasn't any special wing just for first-year electees, with (sniff and sneer) 12th-year eligibles shoved into a back hallway.

You're either a Hall of Famer or you're not.

So I hope the voters will continue to do the right thing now that the first wave of suspected drug cheats has arrived. This is the punishment that fits the crime, and it must be tormenting McGwire every day. What must it feel like to be this close to baseball immortality, close enough to almost feel the doorknob to the Hall of Fame gripped firmly in your hands, only to see it rapidly draw away from you like one of those hallways that stretch out to infinity in some horror thriller?

107

Several years ago, I foolishly allowed my Baseball Writers' Association membership to lapse (though I am now back in good standing), so I still have a few years to go before I am eligible to vote for the Hall of Fame. But if I had a vote, I would have left him off my ballot. And unlike some of my colleagues, it would not have been a temporary thing.

He does not deserve to be in baseball's honored class. He does not deserve to have his statue among the St. Louis baseball immortals in front of Busch Stadium. And while we're at it, I'm still quite puzzled why his name is still on road signs. What I wish the city and state politicians would do is pass a resolution to take the signs down until—or if— he can clear his name of any wrongdoing.

If he doesn't want to talk about his questionable past, then we shouldn't waste any more time honoring it, either.

SHOULD THE CARDINALS RETIRE WILLIE McGEE'S NUMBER?

27 One of the most charming designs inside the year-old Busch Stadium is the graphic images and bold block numbers of all the retired jerseys of Cardinals legends that line the padded green outfield walls. These numbers and images carry the weight of history and the pure romance of St. Louis' most beloved boys of summer.

Yet there is a name, a face, and a number that seems to be missing from this gallery of stars: No. 51, Willie McGee.

McGee might be the most popular Cardinal in the history of the organization. He may not be the greatest Redbird, but he is arguably the most beloved. So beloved, in fact, that Tim McKernan, morning talk show host on KFNS radio, started an online petition last year that now includes more than 7,500 signatures. McKernan's grass-roots movement seemed to have a big impact initially, when a city full of McGee lovers kept logging on to McKernan's InsideSTL.com website and pledging their allegiance to the heart and soul of those 1980s championship teams by purchasing "Retire 51" T-shirts and joining the petition.

Most smart baseball loyalists fully understand that McGee's career probably falls just shy of Hall of Fame consideration. But this isn't about raw statistics. This is about pure love and affection, and sometimes that means a lot more.

How do we know that it's the right thing to retire McGee's No. 51? It's a matter of checking your baseball heart and soul. Here's the simple test: Is there any other ex-Cardinal without a retired number who would cause a minor fan revolt if the Cardinals gave out his number to some kid fresh up from the AAA farm in Memphis?

Imagine the anger, resentment, and incredible outrage that would ensue if the Cardinals dared to give out No. 51 to any new arrival in St. Louis. There is no other Redbird out there who can generate that sort of passion. There's no other former Card who elicits such deep love and respect. It's time to put his name on the wall.

WHO'S THE BEST ALL-TIME CARDINALS MANAGER:

Whitey, Red, or Tony?

28 When a franchise has won 10 World Series stretching over two centuries, six decades, and six managers, trying to decide which of the field leaders is the superior manager is a demanding task.

In St. Louis, defining who belongs on the top dugout step is a rather subjective process.

Is it about results?

The credentials of the Cardinals managers over the years are about as impressive as any franchise in major league baseball history. Red Schoendienst won two NL pennants and one World Series in the 1960s, but also holds the franchise record for most managerial victories with 1,041 and is already in the Hall of Fame as a player/manager. It doesn't seem fair to keep Schoendienst in this argument, however, primarily because despite all those managerial victories, Red's teams finished first only twice in his 12 years as the Cardinals field boss.

Whitey Herzog led the 1980s Cards to three NL pennants

and one World Series, and is easily the fan favorite because of his "good ol' boy" charms and his exciting managerial style.

Then, of course, there is Tony La Russa, the brilliant outsider. At the start of the 2007 season, La Russa trailed only Schoendienst in Cardinals victories (977), was the third-winningest manager in major league history (2,297), and was one of only two managers in history to win a World Series title in both the American and National Leagues. He's won two NL pennants, one World Series, and taken the Cards into the postseason in 7 of his 11 seasons in St. Louis.

Yet when it comes to St. Louis fans, results don't matter nearly as much as personal preference. And when we say "personal preference," that's just local code for "You're either one of us or you're an outsider."

And the code for too many Cardinals loyalists in regards to La Russa is this: He's a West Coast outsider.

Even with all these glowing accomplishments, will La Russa ever be truly beloved in this town? Can he do enough to raise his stature to the same hero-worship level of Whitey?

La Russa has spent 11 seasons in St. Louis being constantly questioned, never universally beloved, and at times downright despised. He has heard the nasty, unreasonable critics and the mean-spirited and hateful "fans," and has probably privately wondered on more than a few occasions if these loud and obnoxious voices were a babbling minority or a populace voice.

I remember what it was like for him during the 2006 World Series. Even in the middle of his finest hour, the idiot fringe rose up and actually demanded that La Russa either resign or be immediately fired because he didn't press the issue of having Kenny Rogers kicked out of Game 2 when the Tigers pitcher was caught with a foreign substance on his pitching hand.

It was typical of the peculiar relationship La Russa has endured with this town. Because he has always been such an intense, cool customer with his dark shades, his hard-pushing personality, his California roots, and his no-nonsense attitude, La Russa is the sort of man who will always be more respected than beloved in St. Louis. He'll always have to deal with the unpardonable sin of not being the lovable Whitey Herzog.

St. Louis transplants always are mystified by this perpetual obsession with all things Herzog. The locals love his good ol' boy buzz cut hairdo, his crusty midwestern charm, and his local roots (born Dorrel Norman Elvert Herzog on November 9, 1931, in New Athens, Illinois). But most of all, they still pine for Herzog's exciting "Whiteyball" managerial style, which emphasized speed, pitching, and tight defense.

For all this Herzog obsession, you would have thought he was responsible for five or six titles and a dynasty under the arches. But Herzog's teams won two NL pennants and one World Series, and his final three teams in St. Louis were a combined 22 games under .500.

113

Because the Cardinals went 24 years between World Series titles, however, this city clung to that 1982 world championship and gave Herzog's legacy a nostalgic boost.

But if we can truly put aside all the nostalgic emotions and preferable personalities, this argument about the Cardinals' greatest all-time manager wouldn't even be about La Russa versus Whitey.

It would actually be about La Russa vs. Billy Southworth, who piloted the "Swifties" dynasty of the early 1940s to three consecutive NL pennants and two World Series championships. In that three-year span, the Redbirds won more than 100 games in back-to-back-to-back seasons. To this day, only three teams in major league history have accomplished that feat. Southworth's "Swifties" won 316 of 462 regular-season contests, and were arguably one of the best teams in baseball history.

But Southworth did not stay in St. Louis very long. After the 1945 season, he left the Cardinals to manage the Boston Braves when he got a hefty $50,000 a year offer. So his brief tenure in St. Louis eliminates Southworth from contention. That leaves us with La Russa, who has been in St. Louis more than 11 seasons. His managerial résumé proves his genius. Only La Russa and Sparky Anderson have managed teams to World Series titles in both leagues. La Russa ranks third in baseball history in most career regular-season victories by a manager, as well as third in most postseason victories by a manager. In his 11 seasons in St. Louis, the Cardinals have finished ranked in first place all but four times.

I'll give La Russa the edge over Herzog not only because of his longevity, which will ultimately send him to the Hall of Fame when he retires, but because of his superior productivity—more victories, more division titles (6–3).

WHO IS THE MOST HATED CHARACTER IN ST. LOUIS BASEBALL HISTORY?

29 Let's face it, no name conjures up more visceral anger and dreadful flashbacks than the infamous umpire who many St. Louis baseball fans firmly believe cost the Cardinals the 1985 World Series: Don Denkinger.

We'll decide later on in the book whether Denkinger really was to blame for the 1985 World Series loss. But for the time being, we'll suspend logic and go with the gut. And the gut says this guy is hated by more men, women, and children in St. Louis than anyone before or after "The Bad Call."

During Game 6 of the World Series, the Cards were seemingly in control, up on the AL champion Kansas City

Royals, three games to two. In the eighth inning, the Cards were leading 1–0 when Jorge Orta came to the plate in the top of the ninth inning to face Redbirds reliever Todd Worrell. Orta hit a slow roller to first baseman Jack Clark, who tossed the ball right into Worrell's outstretched mitt as he covered first base.

Even though everyone in old Busch Stadium could see the play—not to mention millions of TV viewers watching the replays on the national broadcast—first-base ump Denkinger called Orta safe. Denkinger would later admit that he blew the call. But it was too late to do any good for the Cards, who completely unraveled after the play with a series of mental and physical breakdowns. The Royals rallied to win the game.

The next night in Kansas City, crew chief Denkinger worked home plate for Game 7, and it made Cardinals manager Whitey Herzog even more furious than he was the night before. The team lost its composure and was blown out 11–0. The Royals won the World Series, and Denkinger will forever be the ultimate villain in St. Louis.

SHOULD EVERYONE STOP BLAMING DON DENKINGER FOR THE CARDS LOSING THE 1985 WORLD SERIES?

30

Yes.

"Wait a minute, didn't you just tell us he's the most hated guy in St. Louis sports history?"

Yes.

"So how can you turn around and let him off the hook for the fiasco of the 1985 World Series just like that?"

Be patient. We will explain.

The most natural reflex for any Cardinals fan is to blame Denkinger for everything from the Lindbergh baby kidnapping to bad rap music, not to mention the horrific collapse of the Cardinals in the 1985 World Series. We know this because more than 20 years later, he is still Public Enemy No. 1 in St. Louis, the most despised figure in the rich history of this town.

As mentioned elsewhere, no one can argue that Denkinger made the most controversial call in World Series history when, in the ninth inning of Game 6 of the 1985 World Series, Denkinger called the Kansas City Royals' Jorge Orta safe at first base on a play that everyone in the baseball universe could see (because of TV replays) was out.

Does Denkinger deserve *SOME* of the blame for what happened to the Redbirds? Absolutely, but we're about to tell you why as much as you hate this guy, it's time to let it go.

It wasn't *ALL* his fault. He did have help, and there are several more significant reasons why the Cards blew the 1985 World Series. Here they are:

6. VINCE COLEMAN DIDN'T PLAY.

You can't win the big one without your most important weapon, and the Cardinals were already without their most important player before the World Series started.

Speed was Vince Coleman's calling card. The whippet-quick Cardinals outfielder was regarded at the time as the fastest man in baseball. He was the NL's top base-stealer with world-class sprinter speed. Yet Coleman never got on the field in the 1985 World Series because just before Game 4 of the NL championship series, a mechanical tarp that was stored below the artificial turf at old Busch Stadium came out of an underground well and unexpectedly began rolling, at two miles an hour, toward Coleman.

The unsuspecting outfielder never saw it coming, and the freak accident mangled his leg. Suddenly the rookie who stole 110 bases in the regular season was out of the lineup for the Fall Classic.

Coleman could have made a difference in the World Series. Strike that . . . . He *would* have made a difference in the World Series. He was the catalyst of Whitey Herzog's blazing offense, a feared spark plug who got on base, and then created tension and commotion the moment he took those first anxious steps off the bag.

But without him in the lineup, the Cardinals offense stalled.

5. THE CARDINALS STOPPED HITTING.

In the regular season, the Cardinals led the National League with a .264 batting average. When they got into the World Series, their batting average dropped to .185, the lowest ever for a seven-game World Series until the Yankees hit .183 in the 2001 World Series.

Without Coleman in his familiar leadoff position, outfielder Willie McGee, the NL batting champ with a .353 regular-season average, dropped to only .259. Tommy Herr, who led the team with 110 RBI in the regular season, didn't drive in a single run in the World Series. The silent Redbird bats produced only 13 total runs, an all-time low for a seven-game series, scoring only once in the final 26 innings of the series.

Even if they had actually won Game 6, the Cardinals would have been outscored by the losing Royals for the series, 15–13. You can't blame Denkinger for that.

4. BASEBALL OUGHT TO HAVE INSTANT REPLAY.

I know what the baseball purists will say. They'll tell you that part of the magic of baseball is human error. They'll tell you that unlike football, baseball doesn't allow technology to gum up the works.

Then they'll come up with some dreamy poetry about the emerald chess board, the rhymes and rhythms of life and baseball.... yada, yada, yada... blah, blah, blah.

And I will say that there's a place for high technology in baseball, and this was that quintessential moment: If baseball had used instant replay in 1985, Don Denkinger would be off the hook for the Redbirds' defeat, and he'd still be able to get a nice meal in St. Louis without worrying that someone in the kitchen peppered his mashed potatoes with crushed glass.

To all you baseball romantics, calm down. I am not advocating the complete high-tech overthrow of your timeless pastoral delights. I don't want to see instant replay used for balls and strikes (an unmanageable situation to say the least). But don't tell me that baseball couldn't use a little replay booth for vital plays on the base paths or to help judge whether a ball is fair or foul, a home run, or a ground rule double.

Instant replay wouldn't spoil the purity of the game. No, instant replay would help eliminate the easily correctable ineptness in the game.

3. THE CARDINALS LOST THEIR MINDS.

As bad as Denkinger's call was, the way the Cardinals reacted to it was shameful, inexcusable, and dare we say it... choking.

From manager Whitey Herzog right on down the roster, this team lost its composure in the aftermath of that bad call and never regained it. It began like a nervous breakdown, beginning with Herzog blaming Denkinger for the loss in the Game 6 press conference.

Maybe if Herzog had minimized the impact of the call, it would have sent a message to his players not to use Denkinger as a cop-out. But rather than concentrating on going to KC and trying to win this series on the road, the Cardinals dwelled on the call and it got into their heads. Herzog would get himself ejected from Game 7's 11–0 blowout loss by Denkinger. When reporters wondered why the manager would get so lathered up as to get expelled from the seventh and deciding game of a World Series, Whitey's only explanation was, "I've seen enough!"

Then the meltdown seemed to carry over to the players. When Game 7 starter John Tudor was removed from the game after surrendering five earned runs and four walks in 2 ⅓ innings, he stormed into the visitors' clubhouse and punched an electric fan with his pitching hand, suffering a severe cut. Relief pitcher Joaquin Andujar lost his cool after Denkinger called two straight walks on him, going into a frothing rant that got him ejected as well. The biggest surprise was that the Cards only lost by 11.

2. THE CARDINALS DEFENSE WAS HORRIBLE.

We have to continue to emphasize that the Cards blew this. They blew it with lost composure and they blew it with bad bats and worse gloves. Shortly after the horrible

121

Denkinger call, Royals first baseman Steve Balboni hit a pop-up behind first base. Cardinals catcher Darrell Porter called for it... then yelled that he didn't have it.

By that time, Redbirds first baseman Jack Clark was hopelessly out of position to make the catch, and the ball fell harmlessly between them. Porter later would get his signals mixed up with pitcher Todd Worrell, who thought when the catcher was wiping sweat off his face that he was actually giving him the sign for a changeup. He wasn't, so Porter was not prepared for the pitch and he allowed a passed ball.

These little mental transgressions are the things that separate contenders from pretenders. The ability to stay cool under pressure is the first sign of a champion.

1. THE KANSAS CITY ROYALS WERE BETTER.

This just in: Maybe the Royals were just better than the Cardinals.

That's the toughest pill to swallow, isn't it?

One of the most reliable truths in sports is that the best team usually wins a seven-game series. The Royals lost Games 1 and 2 at home, yet still managed to win the World Series. They did it with strong pitching. They did it by not losing their cool. They did it by not blaming the umps, the tarp, the wind, the sun, the moon, or the stars.

BUILDING THE CARDINALS DREAM TEAM

The trouble with picking the greatest Cardinals of all time is that this franchise's history is so rich in talent that it's unfair and impossible to restrict the debate to one man, one position.

So the simple solution is to go with the best Cards of all time, and for that I leaned on the dean of St. Louis sports writers, *Post-Dispatch* baseball columnist Rick ("The Commish") Hummel, a 2006 Hall of Fame inductee, for plenty of advice. With Hummel's help, we extracted this list from his Top 25 of Cardinals greats (minus the four managers).

31 STARTING PITCHER: BOB GIBSON

There was never a better pitcher in the history of the franchise than Bob Gibson. Gibson was so good, so intimidating, so relentless in his pursuit of dominating the opposition that he wouldn't even have a conversation with an opposing player if they met in a restaurant between games.

A young Dusty Baker found that out early in his career with the Atlanta Braves, when one night he and several teammates saw Gibson in the same restaurant. Hank Aaron knew Gibson's no-fraternization reputation, but the kid Baker didn't. So Aaron and another teammate played a cruel joke on him. "Why don't you go over and say hello?" they told Baker.

So Dusty took his wife with him and approached Gibby.

After being quite cordial to Baker's wife, he spun around and snarled at young Dusty Baker, essentially telling him to never speak to him again in public. Thirty-some odd years later, Baker finally met the retired Gibson on more friendly terms and they began recalling that night. "Why were you so mean to me?" Baker asked.

"Hell, I was polite to your wife. What else do you want?" Gibson laughed.

That was just part of the intimidating magic of the man who had a 7–2 career won–loss record in the World Series with a 1.89 ERA, and was completely in a season-long zone in 1968 with his 22–9 record and 13 shutouts, 268 strike-outs, and the unheard-of 1.12 ERA. He had a 95-inning stretch where he gave up only two earned runs. In the 1968 World Series, Gibson set a record with 17 strikeouts in a Game 1 victory, and he pitched in eight straight complete World Series games. And let's not forget that he won the Cy Young and NL MVP.

32 STARTING PITCHER: STEVE CARLTON

Gibson was the greatest pitcher in the franchise. Carlton was its finest left-hander. He was only in St. Louis seven seasons, but in watching the young version of

Steve Carlton (ages 20 through 26 in St. Louis) it was already evident that he was going to be one of the special ones. He compiled 951 strikeouts in his short stint here, and it still is one of the more maddening things to know that the Cards let him go to Philadelphia over a lousy $10,000 raise.

The only thing that makes the idea that owner August Busch let Carlton go over a mere $10,000 *worse* is that after bringing in pitcher Rick Wise from the Phillies (who was unhappy with the Phillies because they wouldn't give him a raise, either), Busch eventually ended up giving *him* a $10,000 raise.

Wise ended up earning the same $65,000 that Busch refused to pay to Carlton. How dumb was that?

Carlton wound up in the Hall of Fame. Wise ended up two years later being traded again, this time for outfielder Reggie Smith.

33 STARTING PITCHER: JESSE HAINES

I wish I knew more about Jesse "Pop" Haines, but from everything I've been told and read about him, he was a tough-as-nails athlete very similar in attitude and style to Gibson. The 19-year veteran right-hander pitched for the Cardinals during the 1920s and 1930s. Only Gibson won more games and had more complete games than Haines (210 victories, 209 complete games), who also pitched one no-hitter. In the 1926 World

125

Series, he was 3–1 with a 1.67 ERA, and in Game 3 he not only pitched a shutout, but he also hit a two-run homer to beat the New York Yankees. He was inducted into the Hall of Fame by the Veterans Committee in 1970.

34 STARTING PITCHER: DIZZY DEAN

In his six years in St. Louis in the 1930s, Dean established himself as one of the best right-handers in the game. He showed up in St. Louis briefly in 1930, then returned in 1932 and within two seasons was a major star, posting a 30–7 record with a 2.66 ERA. Dean led the National League in strikeouts four straight years, and followed his 30-victory season with a 28–12 record in 1935. Between 1933 and 1936, Dean won 102 games.

As Hummel points out, Dean could have been even greater if not for the fluke accident during the 1937 All-Star Game. Dean was the winning pitcher in the 1937 All-Star Game, but he caught a line-drive shot off the bat of Cleveland outfielder Earl Averill in the third inning and broke one of his toes. He never let the injury heal properly, and while overcompensating for it he developed a bad pitching delivery. This caused Dean to suffer an arm injury from which he never recovered. He was not the same pitcher after leaving the Cards for the Chicago Cubs the following season.

35 STARTING PITCHER: MORT COOPER

Like Gibson and Dean, Cooper was one of three Cardinals pitchers to have three consecutive 20-win seasons between 1942–44. Cooper won the 1942 NL MVP when he registered a 22–7 record with 10 shutouts and an ERA of only 1.78. It was the lowest ERA in the National League by a right-hander between 1920 and 1967.

36 RELIEF PITCHER: BRUCE SUTTER

Like many other men on this list, Sutter was another Cardinal who helped revolutionize baseball. Though he didn't invent the split-finger fastball, the Hall of Fame reliever popularized its use, and in the following generations the split-finger became a must-have pitch for every major league hurler.

After arm surgery in 1973, Sutter's fledgling career was about to go on the skids. He quickly realized that he was going to have to develop another pitch if he was going to become a major league pitcher. So Sutter began experimenting with a new pitch, the split-finger. By the time he came to the Cardinals in 1981, he was one of the game's best late-inning closers. He had 127 saves as a Cardinal, including a career-high 45 in his final year at Busch.

Sutter played a major role in the 1982 World Series title, earning two saves and a victory against the Milwaukee Brewers. Cardinals fans will always remember the Game 7 save when he won the game by striking out Brewer slugger Gorman Thomas, then got that leaping hug from catcher and World Series MVP Darrell Porter that is in every highlight reel of Sutter's career.

37 CATCHER: TED SIMMONS

Why not Walker Cooper? He was an exceptionally large man for his time (6-foot-3, 210 pounds) and was the brother of pitcher Mort Cooper, who is already on the greatest squad. And he was good: "Big Coop" was a nine-time NL All-Star and a strong defensive catcher. His offense wasn't shabby, either: In 1943 he batted a career-high .318, and was third in the National League in batting and slugging percentage, fifth in RBI, and runner-up in the NL MVP vote to teammate Stan Musial.

But we had to go with Ted ("Simba") Simmons as our choice for the Top 21 Cardinals. He is widely regarded by most Cardinals historians as the best catcher in franchise history. He holds the club record for most home runs by a switch hitter (172), and he boasted a .298 average in his 13 seasons in St. Louis. No Cardinals catcher played behind the plate in as many games as Simmons (1,564), collected as many hits (1,704), hit as many home runs (172), or had as many RBI (929).

38 FIRST BASE: ALBERT PUJOLS

This is easy. If we were picking only one man per position, *El Hombre* has already done enough in his first six years in the major leagues to blow away the incredibly impressive field of legendary Cardinals first basemen, from Jim Bottomley, to Johnny Mize, to Bill White, to Keith Hernandez, and Mark McGwire. I'll get into the statistics later. But for now, I want to tell you a colorful narrative I overheard a few years ago from three old baseball wise guys swapping stories about the young Albert Pujols. It felt like I had wandered into a Ken Burns documentary without all the pretentious intellectual chatter.

"Albert Pujols? That boy's somethin', mmmm hmmm," said the legendary baseball poet laureate Buck O'Neill, his smooth voice humming with the rhythms of a country preacher. "Love watchin' him hit that ball. Mmmm hmmm."

"I just love watching him play," said 74-year-old former Cub and Cardinal George Altman, smiling and shaking his head with delight.

"We used to have a saying about players like Albert," said 67-year-old Lou Brock, the Cardinals Hall of Famer. "'He makes you sweat.' There are plenty of good players out there, but not everyone makes you sweat. . . . You see Albert standing there in the batter's box, and if you're on the other team, you're sweating for fear of what you know he's capable of. That's why I love watching Albert play. He makes you sweat."

The conversation occurred in 2004, three years before O'Neill passed away at the age of 94. These old-schoolers knew what a treat it was to watch Pujols go to work every day with the work ethic of a skilled craftsman.

129

The hard work in the batting cage, weight room, infield, and video room have helped Pujols produce career stats for his first six seasons that are unmatched by anyone in professional baseball history. As great as the depth is at first base for the Cardinals, it tells you just how great Pujols has been that he ranks No. 1 at his position in franchise history. He's already finished second in the NL MVP race twice, and won it once. Believe me, he'll likely win at least two or three more before his career is over.

Pujols is that rare gem who makes you stop, look, and listen whenever he is at the plate. It really doesn't matter if he doesn't look particularly good at the plate on any particular day. With Pujols, you just know when he walks up to the plate it's time to put down whatever you're doing and pay attention, because something loud and exciting could happen.

The corridors of our sports Halls of Fame are filled with the busts of great superstars, but only a few of them have that legendary presence that makes you believe every time the spotlight draws on them, magic could happen. Muhammad Ali had it. So did Reggie Jackson and Michael Jordan. Pujols possesses that rare gift. It's not just about the numbers, which he keeps producing with amazing regularity. It is those sweat-inducing moments like the home run he crushed in Game 5 of the 2005 NL championship series that rattled off the outfield glass in center field in Houston's Minute Maid Park and turned the previously invincible Astros reliever Brad Lidge into a vulnerable human.

I won't waste any time with rattling off Phat Albert's gaudy stats because he's still building on them as I write this. And really, do I *need* to waste any time with numbers to state Pujols's case as the best first baseman in Cardinals history?

Any questions?

I didn't think so.

39 FIRST BASE: MARK McGWIRE

I'll put my politics aside for a moment and give Big Mac his due. If you can turn your back on his obvious performance-enhanced flaws (I've already stated my case that I think he's an unrepentant cheat), I will as well.

In less than five seasons in St. Louis, based on pure stats—and his impact on the rebirth of baseball during the 1998 season—it's hard to argue against McGwire. In that amazing summer of baseball love, McGwire was a combination of Babe Ruth and P.T. Barnum, banging 70 home runs over major league fences and bringing millions of fans back into the ballparks after their hangovers from baseball's labor mess. During a four-year period between 1996 and 1999, McGwire averaged 61 home runs a season. He broke Roger Maris's 37-year-old single season home run record in 1998 with 70.

I really hate doing this, because I think most of his accomplishments weren't done honestly. The Commish

131

says he belongs on our list, however, so I'll roll with it. But I don't have to like it.

FIRST BASE: JIM BOTTOMLEY

"Sunny" Jim Bottomley was one of those early Hall of Fame players who starred in the 1920s and 1930s for the Cards, and statistically he was one of the best. He led the National League in triples, home runs, and RBI in 1928. In 1924, he drove in 12 runs in one game. He batted over .300 nine times in his 11 seasons in St. Louis. His big seasons were amazing: .371 in 1923, .367 in 1925. He drove in 100 runs six times and had a lifetime batting average of .310. Bottomley just edges out another Hall of Famer, "The Big Cat" Johnny Mize, on this star-studded list of great Redbirds first basemen.

SECOND BASE: ROGERS HORNSBY

Not unlike his Hall of Fame hitting genius contemporary Ty Cobb, Rogers "The Rajah" Hornsby was, as legend has it, one of the most unpleasant, cantankerous men in baseball. But Hornsby's foul attitude did not affect his ability to stroke a bat, which is why he is often regarded as the greatest right-handed hitter of all time.

He had a lifetime batting average of .358, with three seasons of batting averages over .400. The Hall of Famer's .424 batting average in 1924 stands as the highest ever in modern baseball history. Two years after that sterling 1924 season, Hornsby batted .317, drove in 93 runs, and also managed the team to its first NL pennant and World Series title. Hornsby won the NL batting title six consecutive years while with the Cardinals.

This guy had his peculiarities for sure, including his refusal to go to movie houses because he was worried that sitting in the dark to watch a movie would put strain on his eyesight and affect his hitting. You might question his thinking, but you can't discount the results.

 ## SECOND BASE: FRANKIE FRISCH

In 1927, the Cardinals would make a controversial trade that sent Hornsby to the New York Giants, replacing the unpleasant superstar with an even-tempered, well-educated man in Frisch, the "Fordham Flash." Ultimately, the deal turned out to be one Hall of Famer for another.

But Frisch also left the Giants under bad circumstances. Frisch fell out of favor with his manager, John McGraw, who believed his star second baseman dealt the Giants a defeat when he failed to read a sign and cost the team a game-winning run. After the game, McGraw blasted Frisch in front of his teammates and the Flash angrily left the team for several days, forever straining his relationship with the manager. So it was easy to see how this deal to swap the disgruntled All-Stars came together.

Frisch played in eight World Series, four of them (1928, 1930, 1931, 1934) in a Cardinals jersey. This well-educated

133

college man became the perfect steady hand for the wild and crazy "Gas House Gang," who had only one trip to the World Series before he arrived. The longer he was in St. Louis, the easier it became for fans to forget all about the controversial trade of Hornsby. Frisch won the NL MVP award in 1931 with a .311 average, 10 home runs, and 114 RBI, while leading the Cards to the 1931 World Series title over Philadelphia. Two years later, after he became player–manager, he led the team to the 1934 World Series victory over the Detroit Tigers.

43 THIRD BASE: SCOTT ROLEN

The pleasure of watching Scott Rolen at work begins long before the crowds begin filling up Busch Stadium. It begins on that precious little patch of infield dirt hours before the game, when Rolen goes through his intense pregame routines in which he scoops up countless ground balls into his glove.

It is a careful, well-studied ritual designed to sharpen his fielding skills. Balls are hit to his left, to his right, into his chest. Good bounces and bad hops are smacked in his direction in rapid-fire succession, and Rolen rhythmically gobbles up every ground ball. There are other infielders fielding ground balls, but when Rolen does it, it has the fluid feel of a dance. It is a remarkable sight to see a man with roughly the physical dimensions of an NFL tight end move with such grace.

Rolen is one of the best fielding third basemen I've ever seen, and that comes from a guy who grew up watching Brooks Robinson up close and personal perfect the art of playing third base. In the history of the game, only three men immediately come to mind as the premier craftsmen at the hot corner—Robinson, Mike Schmidt, and Scott Rolen. Schmidt (10) and Robinson (16) have more Gold Gloves and are already in the Hall of Fame. But with his seven Gold Gloves, it's a safe bet that Rolen will join them in double digits before long. Only Schmidt has a better blend of the glove and the bat than Rolen, who brings a career .290 average with him. As a five-time All-Star to boot, it's almost automatic to put him on this list.

THIRD BASE: KEN BOYER

Much like first base and the outfield, third base in St. Louis is overflowing with talent. Joe Torre (.308 batting average in five years with the Cards) certainly merited serious consideration, as did Pepper Martin (career World Series batting average of .418), a star for the "Gas House Gang," and Terry Pendleton (.429 as a DH in the 1987 World Series), a favorite of the 1980s crowd.

But Ken Boyer trumps all of them but Scott Rolen. He was the NL MVP in 1964, with a .295 average, 24 home runs, and a league-leading 119 RBI. During a five-year period between 1958–63, he averaged 26 home runs, 98 RBI, and a .304 batting average. His greatest moments as a Cardinal

135

came during that 1964 World Series, when he hit a grand slam in Game 4's 4–3 victory, then had three hits and scored three runs in Game 7's 7–5 championship-clinching victory.

SHORTSTOP: OZZIE SMITH

The best indication of Oz's popularity nationwide was that no other player in NL history has received as many All-Star votes (27,597,904). He has 13 straight Gold Gloves and was inducted into Cooperstown in 2002. There are other famous names at this position that deserve mentioning: Marty Marion, Dal Maxvill, Dick Groat, and Leo Durocher. But none of these men are in the same class with Ozzie Smith, the best fielding performer of all time at his position.

OUTFIELD: STAN MUSIAL

Stan "The Man" could have made this team as a center fielder, left fielder, or right fielder. The greatest living Cardinal was a first-ballot Hall of Famer in 1969 and was the first Cardinal to have his jersey number (#6) retired.

He won seven NL batting titles, had 10 seasons with at least 100 RBI, was chosen to play in 24 All-Star Games, had more than 3,000 hits, crafted a lifetime batting average of .331, and in 1948 batted .376, with 39 homers and 131 RBI, missing out on the Triple Crown by one home run.

My greatest wish is for the Cardinals to give him a better looking statue in front of Busch Stadium, something that actually looks like him (see Argument #82). That's the least the greatest living Cardinal deserves.

47 OUTFIELD: LOU BROCK

Fans voted Brock the left fielder on the All-Busch Stadium team as part of the closing ceremonies for the old stadium in 2005. Speed thrills. Brock took on the very difficult task of replacing a legend when he arrived in St. Louis and moved into left field to replace Stan Musial. He did not disappoint, either.

When you're asked to replace Stan "The Man," knowing that you are an unproven player acquired for a pitcher who had been quite efficient for the Cards (Ernie Broglio), you could easily break under the pressure. Instead, Brock flourished. His batting average jumped from the .251 he posted with the Cubs to .348 as the Redbirds' leadoff hitter the rest of the season, which helped propel the Cards into the 1964 World Series.

48 OUTFIELD: JOE MEDWICK

Joe Medwick is another Hall of Famer in the crowded outfield. The Joe Medwick résumé is about as extensive as you can find. A quick rundown makes it easy to see what he's doing here. He was the last Triple Crown winner in baseball (1937). He was a 10-time

NL All-Star (1934–1942 and 1944), the NL MVP (1937), and the NL batting leader (1937). He was a two-time NL hits leader (1936 and 1937), a three-time NL total bases leader (1935–1937), and NL doubles leader (1936–1938). He led the National League in triples (1934), in home runs (1937), and was a three-time RBI leader (1936–38). The stats sheet on Medwick is almost endless. Here are more big numbers:

- 20-Home Run Seasons: 3 (1935, 1937, and 1938)
- 30-Home Run Seasons: 1 (1937)
- 100 RBI Seasons: 6 (1934–1939)
- 100 Runs Scored Seasons: 6 (1934–1938 and 1941)
- 200 Hits Seasons: 4 (1935–1937 and 1939)

The only downside to Medwick is the discovery that his nickname originally wasn't "Ducky." According to most baseball historians, his original nickname was actually "Ducky-Wucky," earned because of the way he waddled when he walked. But a man can't have a name like "Ducky-Wucky" and still be a part of the gruff and outlandish "Gas House Gang," can he? Then again, I guess his career .324 average might make up for the goofy nickname.

OUTFIELD: ENOS SLAUGHTER

According to his mythology, "Country" Slaughter became the embodiment of hustle on the field as a result of an incident in the minor leagues in 1936 while playing in Columbus, Georgia. As the story goes, Slaughter did not hustle up to the standards of his manager, Eddie Dyer, who proceeded to lay him out verbally.

Slaughter claimed that one moment shaped his belief that the game should always be played full bore, and he vowed never to loaf on a ball field again. His newfound commitment made him one of the game's greatest hustlers. That hustling persona became part of his legend when he made his famous "mad dash" home from first base on Harry Walker's double, which allowed the Cardinals to beat the Red Sox in the 1946 World Series.

As fine a player as he was on the field, he also had a reputation as a bad guy and bigot. He is believed to be one of the Cardinals players who tried to organize a players strike against Jackie Robinson in May of 1947, the first month of Robinson's historic first season as the first black man to play in modern major league baseball. But his on-field accomplishments keep him on this list, despite his foul reputation.

50 OUTFIELD: WILLIE McGEE

If Musial is the greatest Cardinal, than McGee could very well be the most popular—at least among any Redbirds fans old enough to have witnessed the great Whitey Herzog teams of the 1980s. I will always remember that misleading bow-legged, pigeon-toed gait of his that made him seem so passive right before he sprang into action like a blurring whippet. He was a two-time NL batting champ whose humble manner made everyone love him. Now, if we could just get his jersey retired.

OUTFIELD: JIM EDMONDS

We're down to the last spot on the Cardinals Top 21, and the outfield is crowded with legitimate contenders. So it begs the question: Why not? Why not Pepper Martin (.298 avg.)? Why not Curt Flood (seven Gold Gloves)?

The edge goes to Edmonds because he has more Gold Gloves than Flood (eight to seven) and his power numbers (more than 350 homers and nearly 1,100 RBI) are better than both Martin and Flood. But in fairness to Edmonds, he is the best showman to ever patrol the outfield in Busch. What made Edmonds so much fun to watch was his flair for the dramatic and his speed and athleticism.

Athletically, I'd say he is the best center fielder to ever work for the Cardinals. He could track down any ball in the outfield with his speed, or climb the wall and swipe opponents' home runs off the top of the center field wall. At his best, Edmonds gave the Cards a stylish blend of power and batting average from the left-handed side of the plate. His .288 career average in St. Louis was highlighted by three seasons with a .300 average or better, including the 2004 season when he batted .301, tied his career high in home runs (42), and drove in a career-high 111 RBI. Add in those eight Gold Gloves and four All-Star Game appearances, and you can see why Edmonds belongs on this list.

FOOTBALL
FEVER

WHO WAS MORE RESPONSIBLE FOR THE RAMS' SUPER BOWL VICTORY:

Dick Vermeil or Mike Martz?

52 Here's what I want you to do right now: Sit down. I don't want you to be too shocked when you hear the answer to this question.

Offensive coordinator Mike Martz deserves more credit for the Rams winning Super Bowl XXXIV than head coach Dick Vermeil. Yeah, I just said it, and I honestly believe it. And now if you can get over your blood-boiling hatred for Mad Mike for just a few moments, allow me to explain.

For his entire controversial seven-year stay in St. Louis, Mike Martz was always this combustible mixture of unswerving pride and genius, arrogance and attitude, boldness and bravado. Even though he was a vital reason for the Rams' two trips to the Super Bowl, most folks viewed him in a similar light to Cardinals manager Tony La Russa. He was perceived as an arrogant outsider who could never do quite enough to erase the unpardonable sin of not being the beloved former coach.

There was always something about him that they just couldn't love and refused to embrace. Yet through it all, Martz stood there defiantly defying convention, always doing it his way. It is what always intrigued me about Martz. He was a man who railed against the status quo and broke convention with the zeal of a mad genius.

Ultimately, it was his greatest strength that proved to be his most obvious weakness, and what led to his firing after the 2005 season.

But before you curse his memory, you ought to praise it just a bit. Do you remember what that Rams offense looked like in 1998, the year before he arrived to fix it? The Rams were 4–12 and Vermeil looked a lot like a coach on the hot seat. His punchless offense was led by quarterback Tony Banks, an indifferent pro who once admitted that he really didn't like football. In 1998, the Rams were outscored 378–285. Their leading rusher gained 313 yards. Their passing attack accounted for 183 yards a game. They only scored 30 points or more four times.

In 1999 under Martz's guidance, and with an Arena League quarterback no one knew named Kurt Warner, the Rams turned into an NFL superpower. Martz's offense averaged 401 yards a game, scored 526 points, and their 17.8-point margin of victory was the third highest in the NFL since 1950. In 1999, the Rams scored 30 points or more 13 times. In their 23–16 Super Bowl XXXIV victory over Tennessee, Martz's offensive play calling was responsible for Warner's Super Bowl record 414 passing yards. To Vermeil's credit, what we know now that we didn't know then was how he was the steady hand that harnessed and properly directed Mad Mike's Xs and Os genius.

But we saw what Vermeil's offense looked like when he didn't have Martz around. He never got the Rams to the Super Bowl without Martz, but Martz got to another Super Bowl without Vermeil. So, on balance, I think Vermeil needed Martz more than Martz needed him.

WHO WAS MORE RESPONSIBLE FOR THE RAMS' SUPER BOWL LOSS:
Mike Martz or Bill Belichick?

If only we had known then what we know now, maybe we would have been kinder to Mike Martz for his part in the so-called "upset" in Super Bowl XXXVI against the New England Patriots.

Back then, none of us knew that the kid quarterback for the Pats, Tom Brady, was Joe Montana in training. But most of all, back then none of us knew that Patriots head coach Bill Belichick was a young coaching genius with an arsenal of defensive Xs and Os that would over the years ruin the most elaborate offensive game plans from here to Indianapolis, from Denver to Dallas.

But back then, the Rams were 14-point favorites and considered one of the surest bets in Super Bowl history. They were an offensive superpower. They were supposed to score a jillion points, and we were going to start writing all these stories about the making of a new NFL dynasty.

Well, as it turned out, that's exactly what we were writing about, we just got the dynasty wrong. The Patriots, not the Rams, were on the verge of dominating the league. Belichick, not Martz, was on the verge of a football revolution. What we know now that we didn't know then was that the Patriots were just starting a lengthy period of championship building and that Belichick had become the smartest man in football right under our noses.

But still, as good as his defensive game plan was, why didn't Martz run Marshall Faulk more when it was so evident that Belichick's game plan was to hammer the Rams' fast receiving corps every time they came off the line of scrimmage?

Right from the start, you could see what Belichick wanted his defense to do. The Rams receivers were pounded on by New England's cornerbacks in an effort to disrupt their timing routes with Warner. The best example of how effective that strategy worked was when Patriots defensive back Otis Smith knocked Torry Holt to the ground, then easily picked off a timing pass thrown in Holt's direction.

Tell me if this doesn't sound familiar: When put into a stressful, championship situation, Martz went Mad Mike on us, abandoned his balanced offensive attack, and went pass crazy.

He should have known better. Martz forgot one of the most reliable statistics for his team's winning success. From the day Faulk arrived until Super Bowl XXXVI, the Rams were undefeated (18–0) when Faulk gained 100 yards rushing. That amazing success rate would end up going up even more over the next seven seasons. The Rams would win 34 straight games and 38 of 39 between 1999 and 2006 when a St. Louis runner gained 100 yards or more on the ground. Yet on that Super Bowl Sunday in New Orleans, Martz called passes on 68 percent of the Rams' offensive plays. This was not so much a product of what the Patriots were trying to do to them. It was what Martz was doing to himself. On the first 39 plays of the game, Mad Mike had Warner attempt 26 passes.

Was Belichick in Martz's head? Did he know that nothing rankled Martz more than facing a coach who wanted to dictate to Mad Mike how the game will be called? Was Belichick actually baiting Martz when he kept five or more defensive backs on the field almost all game long?

The conventional wisdom of football says that at times like this, when the passing lanes are congested with too many defensive backs and linebackers, you have to run the football.

Give the ball to Marshall.

147

During the Rams' eight-game winning streak leading up to the Super Bowl, Martz's game plan had a decent balance of run to pass. He put the ball in Faulk's hands an average of 23 rushing attempts and 29 total touches a game. But on Super Bowl Sunday the rushing attempts dwindled to 17 and the total touches dropped to 21.

Once the Rams fell behind 17–3, Faulk became the invisible man. On that shocking night in New Orleans, it looked like Belichick had done a masterful job of game-planning. As much of a genius as Belichick is, though, he had help on this one. Mad Mike's stubbornness played the bigger role in dooming the Rams.

DID THE RAMS LET KURT WARNER GO TOO EARLY OR TOO LATE?

54 Quarterback controversies have always been a part of the tradition of pro football, regardless of the city. But no city has ever been so polarized as St. Louis was in 2002, when former Super Bowl MVP Kurt Warner's star began fading and Marc Bulger's began rising.

Football in St. Louis was never the same after that.

People took sides. Anger ensued. Soap operas were created. Conspiracies were concocted. So here's where I assume my role of designated media bad guy.

The Rams got this one right. In fact, when they let Warner go after the 2003 season, it was probably too late.

What were the Rams supposed to do after Warner got injured too frequently, threw too many interceptions, fumbled too often, and lost too many football games? Many people in the Rams organization bit their tongues as Warner told the world he was being replaced because he was the victim of religious persecution, not as a result of him becoming a beaten-down, brittle passer who had become too gun-shy. He said his coaches told him the reason he wasn't playing was because he spent too much time reading the Bible.

Let me say this one more time, just in case we're still a little confused: Jesus was persecuted; Warner was benched.

As great as Kurt Warner was for that incredible three-year period (two NFL MVPs, one Super Bowl victory, two NFC championships, with arguably the greatest statistical single season ever by a quarterback), when the Rams released him in the winter of 2004, it wasn't too early. It was actually way too late.

Why? Two big reasons. First, he was no longer the two-time MVP. He was an injury-prone, fumbling shell of his former self. He was exactly what the Rams thought he was when they acquired him—a serviceable, but flawed veteran backup—and his last three years in the league have supported that clearly. He has gone from the top of the quarterback heap to being benched for younger passers in St. Louis (Marc Bulger), New York (Eli Manning), and Arizona (Matt Leinart).

In 2006, Warner opened the season in Arizona with an impressive start, earning NFC offensive player of the week honors after completing 23 of 37 passes for 301 yards and three touchdowns in a 34–27 victory over San Francisco. The good times wouldn't last, however. Two weeks later, in a 16–14 home loss to St. Louis, Warner was booed off the field after throwing three interceptions and fumbling a snap at the St. Louis 18-yard-line with 1:41 remaining. The loss cost him his job; when the Cardinals fell to a 1–3 record, coach Dennis Green benched him.

One of the harshest facts of athletic life is this everlasting truth: The beginning of a young man's career usually signals the end of an old man's livelihood. This is the existence professional ballplayers grudgingly accept the moment they begin their fantastic athletic journeys. Sooner or later, the same revolving door that so easily swept you in will rather abruptly kick you out onto the street to make room for some younger gun eager to get his turn at stardom.

The second reason it was time for Warner to go was that the Warner vs. Bulger controversy was a distraction the team could no longer tolerate. With Warner gone, there were no more weekly ... no, daily ... make that hourly updates on the quarterback controversy. No more looking over the shoulder. No more complaining about deep, dark conspiracies. No more surprise calls to radio talk shows. No more tiresome, divisive speculation. No more sports radio buzz and uninformed, though highly passionate, chat room debates.

The Rams needed to pull the trigger in order to pull the team together. Bulger and Warner had both publicly and privately been urging Mike Martz and Rams management to make a decision. While Warner was a bit more public, vocal, and disruptive, Bulger had also repeatedly asked Martz to hurry up and make a choice, just as long as Martz did it clearly and definitively.

But once Warner was gone, Bulger took over undisputed ownership of the job he believed he earned long ago. He became a two-time Pro Bowler, in addition to becoming one of the top five or six passers in the NFL. He holds the NFL record for the fewest games needed to reach 1,000 completions (45 games), tied Warner as the fastest to reach 15,000 passing yards (56 games), and ranked only behind Hall of Famer Dan Marino for the most passing yards in his first 60 career games (16,233 yards to Marino's 16,342). His 91.3 pass efficiency rating is the fifth highest career pass efficiency rating in NFL history (behind Steve Young's 96.8, Peyton Manning's 94.4, Warner's 93.8, and Joe Montana's 92.3).

151

But most of all, with Bulger as a starter, the Rams would win 17 of his first 21 starts.

Warner got his freedom to pursue a second chance at a career that has gone progressively south since that Super Bowl loss against New England.

He said he wanted to prove to the football world that he still had it. Ultimately, what he proved was the Rams were right. He kept telling anyone who would listen that he was the same guy, the most magical passer the NFL ever saw during his first three seasons as the Rams' starter. He swore he could return to his old form. In fact, he was convinced he never fell off in the first place.

But after three teams and three different coaches benching him for younger men, it's hard for Warner to dispute that something physical or something mental has turned him into a fragile shell of himself.

He said all he needed was a chance.

He had three chances, and each one ended the same way, with him sitting on the bench.

FLASHBACK: SHOULD THE RAMS GO TO THE THROWBACK UNIFORM?

Since we're on the subject of honoring the Rams' history, let's take it a step further. This is important to me. I love the Rams' contemporary uniforms (just as long as they permanently ditch those hideous dark blue pants; and please, please, please, don't *ever* wear the blue-on-blue combination. I'm not playing. I will hurt someone if this ever happens).

But nothing the St. Louis Rams have worn will ever be as cool as the vintage duds of the old Los Angeles Rams. From the 1960s through the late 1970s, the Rams dressed in beautiful simplicity. The clean white road uniforms with the blue shoulder stripes and the blue helmet with the gleaming white horns were perfect old school.

I can still see the Fearsome Foursome in those uniforms. I can still see Roman Gabriel throwing bombs to my man Jack Snow as he raced across the field in his sparkling white No. 84 jersey.

With so many teams returning to throwback uniforms, it would be nice to see the Rams reach back to their glory days and at least once a year break out this crisp and clean football formal wear.

WHAT WERE THE BEST EVER RAMS DRAFT PICKS?

56

4. CHRIS MASSEY:

The crown jewel of the disastrous draft class of 2002, long snapper Chris Massey is one of those unheralded, yet important pieces to the Rams puzzle. A seventh-round pick out of Marshall, Massey is a special teams beast, a reliable snapper on field goals and punts, and an asset as a tough guy who can get into the scrum and make plays. He also has served as an emergency blocking fullback. The best thing about this pick is that despite the many mistakes the Rams made in 2002 with their good early picks (see the next argument), they somehow found this hidden gem deep into the final round (243rd pick out of 261).

3. TORRY HOLT:

Lots of horrendous mistakes were made all up and down the first round of the 1999 draft, and for a change the Rams weren't the ones making them. Tim Couch, Akili Smith, Ricky Williams, David Boston, Cade McNown, and Troy Edwards were all among the busts taken among the top 15 picks in 1999. Luckily, the Rams did not screw up their pick at No. 6. Torry Holt quickly turned into the primary receiving weapon in the Greatest Show on Turf, and has gone to six consecutive Pro Bowls. He is one of the hardest-working and most intelligent receivers in the NFL.

2. STEVEN JACKSON:

The Dallas Cowboys were in desperate need of a go-to running back in the 2004 draft, yet they traded the 22nd pick in the first round to move down 21 slots into the second round to grab running back Julius Jones. The word around the NFL was that then-head coach Bill Parcells was not enamored with the toughness of a bruising tailback from Oregon State named Steven Jackson.

Luckily for the St. Louis Rams, Parcells lacked good judgment, and the Rams reacted quickly. Sitting in the No. 26 position, the Rams made a trade with Denver to move up two slots and grabbed Jackson at No. 24 in the first round. The team was looking for a man to slowly ease into the heir apparent role for all-time great Marshall Faulk, and it worked out perfectly. After a couple of years as an apprentice, Jackson had a breakout Pro Bowl season in 2006, putting together the fifth-best yards-from-scrimmage season in league history with 2,334 yards (1,528 rushing, 806 receiving). The 6-foot-2, 235-pound "Train" is now setting his sights on an NFL record of 2,500 yards from scrimmage. If we do this list again in five years, Jackson will likely be considered the best draft pick ever.

155

1. ORLANDO PACE:

It's not hard to understand why the Rams made the right decision when they packaged four draft picks in 1997 to move up to the No. 1 overall pick and grab Orlando Pace out of Ohio State. Pace has become the anchor on the left side of the offensive line, a seven-time Pro Bowler, and a future Hall of Famer at tackle.

So what did it cost the Rams to acquire Pace? Those four draft picks turned out to be college teammate Shawn Springs, a two-time Pro Bowler at cornerback (first round), nine-year NFL veteran offensive guard Dan Neil (second round), defensive end Terry Day (fourth round), and quarterback and NFL journeyman Koy Detmer (seventh round). Was it worth it? Yeah, you bet it was. Pace is one of the best men to ever play his position, an athletic and powerful mountain that can pile drive you into the ground with those massive arms that feel like jackhammers.

WHAT WERE THE WORST EVER RAMS DRAFT PICKS?

57 5. THE ENTIRE 2002 DRAFT:

Other than the final pick, long snapper Chris Massey, it's impossible to separate any of these wretched picks from 2002 on their own merit. This was the ultimate symbol of the Martz drafting era, a psychedelic blend of mind-altering miscues that provided Rams fans with thousands of man hours of misery and regret.

At the bottom of the first round, the Rams went with UCLA linebacker Robert Thomas, who never amounted to much more than a backup in St. Louis and an ordinary player in Green Bay. In the second round, the Rams chose cornerback Travis Fisher, who was a serviceable starter for a few years. One pick later, however, the New England Patriots took receiver Deion Branch.

In the third round, the Rams went with running back Lamar Gordon, when multi-talented running back Brian Westbrook was still on the board. At the bottom of the third round, they drafted Nebraska quarterback Eric Crouch and immediately turned him into a wide receiver. The only problem was, no one ever asked Crouch if he wanted to play receiver (he didn't), and he kept trying to play quarterback (he couldn't). Things only got worse, with fat and flabby guard Travis Scott, linebacker/defensive end Courtland Bullard, Ohio State quarterback Steve Bellisari (they tried to make him into a safety; another horrid failure), and in the seventh round, the only guy still with the team, Chris Massey.

What makes matters worse for the Rams is what they left on the table. Here are just a few players who the Rams had an opportunity to draft and ignored in 2002: Clinton Portis, LeCharles Bentley, Ladell Betts, Antwaan Randle El, and two players they ultimately signed as veteran free agents four and five years later at much higher prices, Wil Witherspoon and Randy McMichael.

4. TRUNG CANIDATE:

After all this time, we're still scratching our heads trying to figure out why the Rams wasted the 31st pick in the first round of the 2000 draft on the running back Canidate. A year earlier, they made a blockbuster trade for all-world running back Marshall Faulk, so it made no sense to use a first round selection on an average-at-best talent like Canidate, who spent three seasons in St. Louis lost on the depth chart behind Faulk. The Rams would have been much better off using that pick to strengthen the defense. Among the very talented future NFL starters and stars who were still on the board were Jerry Porter, Ian Gold, Mike Brown, and Darren Howard.

3. JACOBY SHEPHERD:

He was drafted in the second round of the 2000 draft as a cornerback out of Oklahoma State, and he did absolutely nothing for the Rams. He was a bust by any definition of the word. He played two seasons for the Rams; in that time, he had no starts, one interception, and two tackles.

2. EDDIE KENNISON:

Eddie Kennison is not a draft bust. He spent 12 seasons playing wide receiver in the NFL after the Rams selected him with the 18th pick in the 1996 draft. He caught more than 500 passes for more than 8,000 yards and 42 career touchdown receptions. All and all, that's not a bad life for a man in the rough and tumble world of pro football.

The only trouble with Eddie Kennison as far as Rams fans are concerned is that he isn't Marvin Harrison.

What makes the Kennison pick one of the worst for the Rams is the simple fact that one pick later, the Indianapolis Colts selected future Hall of Fame pass catcher Harrison. Harrison's NFL contributions make Kennison look like a piker: more than 1,000 career receptions, more than 13,000 yards, and 122 career touchdown catches. He will finish in the top 10 in nearly every significant NFL career pass-catching statistical category, and is regarded as one of the all-time best receivers in the game.

Imagine how many more fireworks the Greatest Show on Turf could have created with a trio of Isaac Bruce, Harrison, and Torry Holt racing downfield to snatch in all those bombs from Kurt Warner.

Sorry Eddie, it's not your fault.

1. LAWRENCE PHILLIPS:

The Rams made one mistake after another in 1996 regarding the state of their running game. First of all, head coach Rich Brooks ran off two-time Pro Bowl tailback Jerome Bettis, trading him away to the Pittsburgh Steelers. Bettis, of course, would go on to the Iron City and become even better, finishing off his future Hall of Fame career in 2005 as one of the top all-time rushers in NFL history.

Next, the Rams put their faith in a troubled running back from Nebraska, Lawrence Phillips, who was far more of a headache than he was worth. Phillips proved to be a constant nightmare for the Rams, gaining 632 and 633 yards, respectively, in his only two seasons in St. Louis. Meanwhile, eight picks later in the first round, the Tennessee Titans drafted Eddie George, a four-time Pro Bowler who ended a nine-year NFL career with more than 10,000 rushing yards.

Phillips, however, only spent parts of three seasons in the NFL. He was cut midway through the 1997 season in St. Louis in a dispute with new head coach Dick Vermeil, and was in and out of trouble with the law over a series of domestic violence incidents. He was sentenced to 20 years in prison in 2006 for several counts of assault with a deadly weapon.

WHO WERE THE WORST EVER DRAFT PICKS FOR THE FOOTBALL CARDINALS?

58 Picking the worst ever football Cardinals draft pick is like finding fleas on a mutt's back. What we have here is an abundance of itches. "We're talking about something like 18 years worth of bad, awful drafts," former Big Red head coach Jim Hanifan chuckled. "You'd think after maybe six or seven years, Bill (Bidwill) would have gotten the message, but he never did."

Hanifan, the Cardinals head coach from 1980 through 1985 after serving as an assistant from 1973 through 1978, was witness to all the dreadful picks and comical mistakes. In 1983, Hanifan sat down with Bidwill and tried to convince him that something was terribly wrong with the way the front office was doing business on draft day. "I told him we really, really have to change the scouting department," Hanifan said. "He just got mad, got up and walked out and everything I said just went in one ear and out the other."

5. STEVE LITTLE:

Who drafts a kicker in the first round? Only the Cardinals. Little was a punter/place kicker who made only 10 career field goals for St. Louis. He also averaged only 38 yards a punt in two seasons.

4. JOHN LEE:

Who drafts a kicker in the second round? Again, only the Cardinals. Lee ended up playing one year in St. Louis, converting a measly eight kicks.

3. KELLY STOUFFER:

The sixth overall pick in the 1987 draft, Stouffer held out for his entire rookie season and never played a down for the Cardinals. In 1988, the Cardinals made a trade with the Seattle Seahawks for Pro Bowl safety Ken Easley. However, typical of the Cardinals' snakebitten ways, Easley failed his physical because of failed kidneys and was forced to retire. As compensation, the Cards got the last thing they needed—more draft picks to screw up.

2. CLYDE DUNCAN:

"I can still remember the day the Cardinals drafted him (1985), and the kid was just as shocked as we were that he was drafted in the first round," said Hanifan. "'I didn't expect to be a No. 1 pick,' he told me. Well, I guess so. I told the owner and our general manager George Boone, our first draft pick can't play. Number one, he can't catch, that's a problem there. He can't run. He couldn't break 4.7 in the 40. And to top it all off, he's chicken. He's afraid to go over the middle. But other than that, he's a nice kid."

1. STEVE PISARKIEWICZ:

"This kid was awful. I'm the guy who finally cut him," said Hanifan. "The day I did it, I told him, 'Well Steve, I gotta give you credit. It took three of us (head coaches) to (finally cut you).' He couldn't throw. He had problems with his eye sight. It was a miracle he was able to play as well as he did on the collegiate level." Hanifan and the rest of the coaches thought the Cards would draft a young linebacker out of New Mexico named Robin Cole, who ended up having a good career in the NFL. And then the announcement came: "The Cardinals select...Steve Pisarkiewicz!" "Well that was it," Hanifan said. "The entire assistant coaching staff got up and left our offices and went to a bar to have a drink. That pick just took the heart and soul out of us."

WHO'S THE MOST HATED MAN IN ST. LOUIS FOOTBALL HISTORY?

59 With his bow ties, skinflint ways, bizarre hires in the front office, flat-out weird draft picks, and of course the team's perennial losing, there is plenty of evidence to make football Cardinals owner Bill Bidwill one of the most hated men in St. Louis sports history.

But Bidwill did not stop there. He moved into the upper echelon of villainy in St. Louis when he decided to relocate the football Cardinals out of St. Louis and into the Arizona desert. Bidwill's carefully orchestrated business move certainly helped him financially, but it also took pro football away from local NFL fans for a decade. As a result, just the sound of his name became one of the more despicable sounds in St. Louis and bow ties the most unpopular fashion statement.

It's hard to decide what made St. Louis hate him so much—the crappy teams he kept giving us or taking the crappy team away from us. In any event, nothing warms the hearts of a vindictive St. Louis sports fan more than seeing the Big Red's misfortunes follow them to Phoenix. Bidwill is a peculiar man who never really had much of a clue about how to build a successful franchise, and in reality did the town a favor by leaving. With his mess out of the way, the Rams were able to come to St. Louis and give us two NFC championships and one Super Bowl victory. That's not a bad tradeoff if you ask me.

I keep wondering who else could come close to the unfettered hatred that Bidwill generated, and the plain truth is no one comes close. Sure, former Rams head coach "Mad Mike" Martz frustrated legions of football fans in this town with his occasionally infuriating play calling. But because he was the genius offensive coordinator who created the Greatest Show on Turf, he gets (what else?) a pass.

NFL DREAM TEAM: CARDINALS OR RAMS

Pick the Best

Part of the problem with picking the best ever NFL squad from St. Louis is that the football Cardinals are sentimental favorites, while the Rams carry the clout of championship production. It's a lot like deciding between a comfortable old shoe or a sassy, stylish new one.

I will tell you this: I harbor no such gushy sentimentality. I am a man who will not be swayed by a childhood of worshipping the football Cardinals. I built this list strictly on raw productivity. All-Stars, MVPs, Pro Bowlers, and playoff veterans only need apply. If that shortchanges the Big Red, so be it. Unlike the chapter that opened this book, the criteria for admission to this list is not vague and ever-shifting. This is not about playing favorites based on which jersey you wore growing up. So here's my list of all-time greatest pro football players in St. Louis history.

60 QUARTERBACK: KURT WARNER

Why not Jim Hart? To most long-time St. Louis football lovers, Hart was the only quarterback they ever knew, quarterbacking the Big Red from 1966 to 1983. He was the NFC Player of the Year in 1974, a four-time Pro Bowler, and he led the Cards to three consecutive seasons of 10 or more victories. In championship-starved St. Louis, those two NFC East titles in 1974 and 1975 were the height of championship success. But Hart was a career 51-percent passer who only twice in his 18 years in St. Louis threw for more than 3,000 yards, and in 12 of those seasons completed more interceptions than touchdowns.

So this is too easy. Kurt Warner is a two-time NFL MVP, a Super Bowl MVP, and a three-time Pro Bowler who put together the greatest three-year period any NFL quarterback has ever had. In his breakout season of 1999, Warner led the Rams to a world title, threw for over 4,353 yards, generated 41 touchdowns, and owned an impossible 109.1 quarterback efficiency rating. He followed that up with

166

3,400 yards and 21 touchdowns in 2000, and an eye-popping 4,830 yards with 36 touchdowns in 2001 to go along with a 101.4 rating and another trip to the Super Bowl. Warner still has the second-highest career pass efficiency rating in NFL history (93.8) and is a career 66-percent passer. This isn't a contest. Warner is a runaway pick. If we wrote this book in another five years, he might have some stiff competition from Marc Bulger, but Bulger would have to take this team to the Super Bowl for that to happen. Until then, Warner is the man.

 ## RUNNING BACK: MARSHALL FAULK

Even as he neared the end of his fantastic football journey, Marshall Faulk was able to conjure up these sweet football flashbacks. There was Marshall Faulk with a football tucked snugly in his arms, and there were all those angry defenders swirling around him. Two to his left, three to his right, four more dead ahead, and every last one of them filled with evil intentions in their violent hearts and souls.

Everybody misses him.

There was still enough magic left in his legs near the end to give us these athletic flashbacks of how extraordinary he was. In his last full season with the Rams (2004), Faulk could no longer sustain a full 16-game season of brilliance. But he did have three 100-yard rushing games to remind us what vintage Marshall could do. On the Rams' first offensive play in a 17–10 season-opening victory over the Arizona

Cardinals, he took a handoff from Marc Bulger on first down and glided to the left. As he danced behind the sizeable rear ends of Chris Dishman and Orlando Pace, Faulk did a little zig to the right, a little zag to his left. Then he down-shifted for a heartbeat, did about three of those herky-jerky, knee-buckling jump stops—every move going in a different direction—and swooshed sideways for a 15-yard gain.

So this is what we were left with at the end, these brief snippets and wondrous quick hits. The last three or four years of his career had basically reduced him to this, playing with various bumps and bruises, a shadow of his brilliant self. He played with all sorts of twisted body parts, including a bum knee that was operated on twice over the course of 11 months, a high ankle sprain that never healed, and a broken hand.

He had a game full of sweet, jaw-dropping bursts of athletic brilliance. He danced and pranced, zigged and zagged, stuttered and strutted all over the place.

He was so good for so long that even his defensive team-mates had to sneak a peak, even when they should have been sitting on the bench getting their rest. Aeneas Williams, the former Pro Bowl defensive back, was asked one day if he was one of those players who felt compelled to watch Faulk run. "That's like asking someone who was standing next to Picasso when he was painting a mural and a fight broke out if he was watching the fight and not watching the masterpiece being created on the wall," Williams said. "Of course I was looking at him. I would never miss it. Watching him run is like seeing a portrait in motion.

"Wouldn't it be great if they could somehow figure out a way to put a paint brush on his feet as he's doing his thing out there? Wouldn't you just love to see what sort of masterpiece would end up on that canvas?"

Why not Cardinals great Ottis Anderson? He was the NFL Rookie of the Year (1979) and rushed for more than 1,000 yards in five of his first six seasons in the league (the only non-1,000-yard season was a strike year). His 1,605 yards rushing as a rookie are better by more than 200 yards over Faulk's best season, and he had only one less 1,000-yard season than Marshall (6).

Yet even though he was a Super Bowl MVP (with the New York Giants), there was never a time when Anderson was regarded as the best running back in the game. Faulk had a four- or five-year run where he was the unquestioned best offensive force in the NFL. He, too, was a Rookie of the Year, added seven Pro Bowls to his résumé, and was the first player in NFL history to gain 2,000 yards from scrimmage in four consecutive seasons. He was named the league MVP once, and was a three-time offensive player of the year. This really is no contest in my book, because without Faulk the Rams don't become the dominant force in the NFC for that breathtaking three-year stretch.

WIDE RECEIVER: TORRY HOLT

This is the toughest position to decide on. When you have a team like the Rams' Greatest Show on Turf that is built around world-class wide receivers, it's challenging to sort through the likes of Isaac Bruce and Torry Holt and come up with the fine margin that separates two Pro Bowl-caliber pass catchers.

Bruce has been at the top of his game for 13 impressive seasons, and ranks high on most career stats with 887 receptions and 13,376 yards. He has compiled eight seasons with more than 1,000 receiving yards and his best season was his second in the league (1995), when he caught 119 passes for 1,781 yards and 13 touchdowns. After his first three seasons, it looked like he was going to be the Rams' go-to guy for the next decade. But injuries kept him out of 15 games over the next two seasons, and in 1999, the Rams drafted Torry Holt with their first-round pick.

Here's why you have to go with Holt. Just look at what Marc Bulger and Kurt Warner did with him. He became their first option on offense in rather quick order. After playing the role of the No. 2 guy as a rookie (52 catches), Holt emerged as the No. 1 man over the last seven seasons, stringing together seven consecutive 1,000-yard receiving seasons and was the reception leader in each of those seasons.

I grew to appreciate Holt even more when he wasn't playing games. I was watching training camp before the

2006 season during another scorching August afternoon when it was so humid you felt like you were breathing under a wet blanket. But watching Holt go through that practice was enlightening, and helped explain why he's so good.

Like so many great players, he does not rely solely on his athletic gifts. It is his work ethic that makes him so good. So there he was running these pass route drills with the precision of a man playing in a two-minute drill in the fourth quarter of a Super Bowl. Every route he ran was exactly as it should be. He made his first break at exactly 13 yards and came back to the sideline marker exactly at 10 yards. He didn't make his cut at 12 ½ yards, or 14 yards, or 11 yards. He didn't come back to 11 yards, or 9 yards, or 12 yards. It was a precise measure and a perfectly choreographed pattern that had been worked on countless times between Holt and Bulger.

He could have slacked off on any one of those practice routes, but he didn't. And that's why he gets the nod here.

63 OFFENSIVE TACKLES: DAN DIERDORF AND ORLANDO PACE

I can't come up with one good reason to pick one over the other, so I will settle for letting a Hall of Fame tackle and a future Hall of Fame tackle share a spot on my ultimate team. Hall of Famer Dierdorf, who played for the Cardinals from 1971–83, was so good he could have made this team from any position on the offensive line. I am convinced that he could have been a Pro Bowl talent at guard or center. In fact, Dierdorf began his career as a guard, moved to left tackle, then right tackle, and played center for part of one season due to injuries. Because of his size, he was able to easily take on the influx of larger nose tackles playing in the new wave of 3–4 defensive fronts.

What you have to love about Pace is that he is one of the least penalized tackles in the NFL. With his size (6-foot-7, 325 pounds) and athleticism, he doesn't have to cheat to crush so many of these blitzing linebackers and speedy defensive ends. There are few offensive linemen who have the outstanding feet and uncanny strength that Pace possesses. When you see his punch move in practice, he literally stuns pass rushers to a full stop. He overpowers most players, and even when his man is elusive enough to get him off balance on his pass-blocking, Pace has the grace of a basketball player and recovers most times to get his big mitts on guys and fend off assaults. These two men are among the very best to play the position in NFL history.

64. OFFENSIVE GUARDS: CONRAD DOBLER AND BOB YOUNG

This is another one of those positions with an abundance of talent. Cardinal Ken Gray was a six-time Pro Bowl guard on some of the best offensive lines in the NFL. He was not a particularly big man (6-foot-2, 245 pounds), but for his day he was a brute. He handled many a future

Hall of Famer on his own, and anyone who watched those Big Red teams back then knew that the best thing they had going were the men on the offensive front. Irv Goode was another stud from that era who deserves consideration.

My personal favorite is Ram Adam Timmerman, a colorful personality. He and his buddy Andy McCollum were known as the "Donut Boys" for their love of Krispy Kreme donuts. But there was a mean streak in Timmerman once the games began, and you could pretty much bet that if there was some sort of skirmish in the trenches, the 6-foot-4, 310-pound 13-year veteran was the instigator. He was a two-time Pro Bowler and helped both the Green Bay Packers (twice) and Rams (twice) to four Super Bowls. Timmerman played in more than 200 games for the Rams, including an iron-man team record of more than 180 consecutive games.

Yet when it comes to offensive linemen in St. Louis, there is no better authority on the subject than Jim Hanifan, the legendary offensive line coach for both the Cards and Rams, and he tells me he would go to war with only two guards on his all-time St. Louis NFL team: two old Cardinals, Conrad Dobler and former All-Pro Bob Young.

Dobler wasn't the greatest player in the world, but he was the toughest. He would play in pain every game, and he would dominate everyone he came up against. He was a tough-as-nails mad man who was considered the dirtiest player in the NFL. But that bad rap never did him justice as

173

THE BEST ST. LOUIS SPORTS ARGUMENTS

Dierdorf's running partner on those outstanding Cardinals offensive lines in the 1970s.

"Bob Young had Hall of Fame ability, one of the best talents I've been associated with in my coaching life," said Hanifan. "He had a pot belly and looked like a banker. But he could run a 4.85 (40-yard dash) and he would drive you off the ball seven yards and then put you on your ass every time."

If they're good enough for Hanifan, they're good enough for me.

65 TIGHT END: JACKIE SMITH

Let's not even try to quibble about this one. There is only one Hall of Fame tight end who has ever stepped onto a football field wearing a St. Louis uniform and that man is Jackie Smith. Don't even think about coming up with a Ram, because in case anyone has forgotten, in Mike Martz's offense tight ends were afterthoughts and casual playthings. They were nothing to be taken seriously. Maybe in about 10 years we will look back at a young tight end from the Scott Linehan era and include him in this debate, but for the time being, why even bother discussing any other tight end in this conversation? When you don't have even *one* other guy who's made so much as an All-Rookie team, an All-NFC team, or even earned one Pro Bowl trip, there's just no point in talking about anyone but Jackie Smith, period. End of conversation.

174

66 CENTER: BOB DeMARCO

Center is another offensive line position rich in talent. Why not Andy McCollum? The anchor of the Rams offensive lines for more than five years, McCollum took an unconventional route to the NFL. He came into the league as an undrafted free agent with the Cleveland Browns, then bounced around on practice squads for the Browns and New Orleans Saints, tossing in a little stint in NFL Europe and the Arena League.

When he finally made his way to St. Louis, it was as a reserve guard on the Super Bowl championship team. He made the switch to starting center a year later, then settled in as the anchor of the line. A physical blocker and intelligent leader, McCollum made all the line blocking calls and was one of the most stable members of an injury-plagued group, putting together a string of more than 140 consecutive starts.

And why not Tom Banks? After all, the Cardinals star made four Pro Bowls in the mid- and late-1970s.

McCollum and Banks were very good. However, according to Hanifan, the best of them all was Bob DeMarco, a three-time Pro Bowler in the 1960s who was a 14th-round draft pick in 1960 out of Dayton. "Lots of good ones, but he's the best," said Hanifan. "Big, strong and smart. He handled some of the best defensive linemen in football, guys who are in the Hall of Fame now."

According to Hanifan, what gave DeMarco the edge is

175

that he played in the pre-expansion NFL, which meant he was playing against a less-watered-down league. Therefore, he faced Pro Bowl and Hall of Fame talent nearly every week.

67 DEFENSIVE LINE: KEVIN CARTER

Why not Curtis Greer? The best defensive pass rusher on the Cardinals teams of the early to mid-1980s (1980 through 1987 in St. Louis), Greer still holds the St. Louis Cardinals team record for single-season sacks with 16 in 1983 and followed it up with 14 in 1984. Overall, in his eight seasons in St. Louis, he had 69 career sacks, though the Cardinals somehow failed to list his 19.5 sacks from his first two NFL seasons in his career sack totals. Yet it's hard to pick Greer as one of the best to ever play in St. Louis when he was never named to a Pro Bowl. So that's why we go with Kevin Carter, who was the best defensive lineman on the Super Bowl championship team and had impressive team-leading seasons of 17 sacks, 12 sacks, and 9.5 sacks in his six seasons (1995–2000) with the Rams. Unfortunately for Carter, who had 62.5 career sacks as a Ram, his most memorable moments in St. Louis involved his public spats over the perceived pay inequity for the defense after the Super Bowl XXXIV victory and that little matter of asking to come out of the final moments of the Tennessee game in 2000 that puzzled Dick Vermeil to no end.

In case you don't remember, during the Titans' final offensive drive, Tennessee was in a hurry-up offense and Carter ran out of gas chasing quarterback Steve McNair all over the field. So with less than a minute to go in the game, a winded Carter took himself out of the game for a breather. Vermeil just kept looking at him and saying, "Are you kiddin' me?"

But Carter was a dominant force, good enough to go to the Pro Bowl as voted by his peers, and his single-season sack total of 17 in 1999 ranks only behind the dominant seasons of Hall of Famers Deacon Jones (five seasons of 18 or more sacks) and Jack Youngblood (18 sacks) when the club resided in Los Angeles.

68 DEFENSIVE LINE: LEONARD LITTLE

What about Grant Wistrom or D'Marco Farr? Sure, they had their moments, but both were merely work-horse kind of guys and valuable complementary components on those Super Bowl teams.

For sustained pass rushing excellence, my money is on Leonard Little, a two-time Pro Bowl selection whose 74 regular-season career sacks are the most by any Rams pass rusher since 1982. In 10 years with the Rams, Little is only 20 sacks away from tying Hall of Fame lineman Merlin Olsen for third on the franchise career sack list. Little has spent the last few years as the team's only major pass

177

rushing threat, which means he battles double and triple teams every game, not to mention all the exotic grabbing, clutching, and behind-the-back tackling that offensive linemen and undersized blocking backs have resorted to in order to keep Little out of the backfield.

By the time he finishes with the Rams, Little will likely rank behind only L.A. Rams NFL Hall of Famers Deacon Jones, Jack Youngblood, and Merlin Olsen as the best pass rushers in team history.

69 LINEBACKER: LONDON FLETCHER

London Fletcher never should have played a down in professional football. He was too small (5-foot-10, 235 pounds). He was undrafted out of a Division III college not exactly known as an NFL factory (John Carroll University). Yet somehow, London Fletcher is still in the NFL, and he was the heart and soul of the Super Bowl defense, leading the Rams in tackles in three of his four seasons in St. Louis. One of the biggest mistakes the Rams ever made was underestimating Fletcher's importance to the defense, letting him go in free agency to Buffalo in 2002. The team has missed his leadership and run-stopping ability ever since. The only other linebacker who comes close is former Cardinals star E.J. Junior (1981–86 in St. Louis), a one-time Pro Bowl inside linebacker (1984) who was one of the few bright spots on the Gridbird defense.

70 CORNERBACK: ROGER WEHRLI

Wehrli spent his entire 14-year career with the Cardinals and was probably the first player given the designation of "shutdown corner," according to Hall of Fame quarterback Roger Staubach, who swears Wehrli was the best cornerback he ever faced. Speed was Wehrli's best weapon, and the seven-time Pro Bowler had 40 career interceptions. The Hall of Famer was also named to the NFL's All-Decade team for the 1970s. No one messed with this guy, and those that were foolish enough to do so usually wished they didn't. There aren't a lot of Cardinals who can find their way onto the All-NFL squad for St. Louis, but Wehrli was one of those automatic picks that go without hesitation. Though there have been some other decent cornerbacks who have played in St. Louis, there's no one even close to belonging in the same Hall of Fame discussion with Wehrli.

71 SAFETY: LARRY WILSON

The only other man who merits consideration in this conversation at safety is Rams safety Aeneas Williams, who will likely join Wilson in the Hall of Fame in the next few years. Williams is an eight-time Pro Bowler at both cornerback (seven times) and safety (one). Williams was named to the NFL's All-Decade team for the 1990s at cornerback. He made a seamless conversion to safety when he came to the Rams from the Arizona

Cardinals. After two seasons at cornerback, in 2003 Williams became a safety, had four interceptions, and scored two touchdowns: one on a 46-yard interception return, and the other on a 90-yard fumble recovery.

But his two seasons at safety are not enough to crowd out the great Larry Wilson, who became the innovator of the safety blitz, was an eight-time Pro Bowler, and became a six-time All-NFL player. Wilson played all 14 years in St. Louis with the Big Red. Wilson is an easy choice.

72 KICKER: JEFF WILKINS

Why not Jim Bakken? The former Cardinals kicker holds the NFL record for most field goals attempted (9) and made (7) in a game. But he falls far short in that he really wasn't a very accurate kicker. He only made 287 out of 447 career field goal attempts (67 percent) and 534 extra points out of 553 tries.

When you break down his kicking reliability, Bakken made 51 of 71 from 20 to 29 yards, 50 of 68 between 30 and 39 yards, 40 out of 85 between 40 and 49 yards, and was a career 0-for-9 beyond 50 yards. Now compare that with the Rams' Mr. Money, Jeff Wilkins. He is a career 82.5 percent place kicker, and has only missed one extra point in 10 years with the Rams (99.4 percent). When you look at everything Wilkins does, he ranks higher than Bakken. He's outstanding from long distance (73 of 110 between 40 and 49 yards; 23 of 32 beyond 50 yards). Inside the 30,

Wilkins has only missed three career field goals in 107 attempts. There's a very good reason why Wilkins's nickname is "Money." He does not miss.

73 PUNTER: SEAN LANDETA

Landeta punted in the NFL for 21 years, and is the league's all-time yardage leader. In his two separate stints with the Rams (four years total) he averaged 44.3 yards, 44.8 yards, 42.8 yards, and 43.3 yards. He should end up in the Hall of Fame, but it's hard for punters to get the necessary votes. But there ought to be some consideration for a man who has been able to remain an effective punter at age 43. Plus, you gotta love a guy who parlayed being a punter in New York into dating Penthouse models.

74 ALL-AROUND ATHLETE: TERRY METCALF

Okay, I admit it, I bent my own rules with a little friendly persuasion from my colleague Bernie Miklasz, the long-time *Post-Dispatch* columnist and Pro Football Hall of Fame voter. "You gotta find a spot on this team for Metcalf," he told me. "I don't care how you do it, even if you have to make up a position for him, get him on the team."

Since Bernie's been covering pro football in this city longer than anyone I know, I was willing to do it. Besides,

Metcalf (who played with the Cards from 1973–77) has always been one of my favorite players, too. This is all you need to know as to why the running back/return man belongs on this squad: In the 14-game 1975 season, Metcalf set the NFL record for combined yards with 2,462. To better understand how big a deal this was, over the last 22 years, only one other NFL player has topped that total, and it took San Diego Charger Lionel James 16 games to do it.

SINGING THE BLUES

IS BEING A BLUES FAN AS FRUSTRATING AS BEING A CUBS FAN?

75 Being a Chicago Cubs fan takes a certain perverse devotion and blind ignorance of a century's worth of heartbreak. There isn't a day that goes by when a Cubs fan doesn't see all the evidence in front of him as to how miserable and doomed his Cubbies are, yet a Cubs fan is always heartbroken, crushed, and shocked when by the beginning of August there is no chance for even a sniff of the postseason.

To be a Cubs fan, you need to develop a certain blind spot for danger. The best way to describe your annual optimism going into another baseball season is this: You will walk into a dark alley, hear the dogs barking, see the flash of a fired gun, listen to several shrill screaming voices of desperation, and somehow be shocked, *shocked I tell you*, when you get mugged.

But to be a true Blues hockey fan in St. Louis requires a different kind of optimism, because a Blues fan actually has historical good reasons to be optimistic. A Blues fan's justification for getting his hopes up is based on the evidence that this franchise has had more than its fair share of outstanding moments in sports history. The only trouble with being a

Blues fan is to know that, historically, those giddy highs will almost always be followed by tear-your-guts-out-and-slide-them-on-a-jagged-shard-of-glass disappointments.

To be a Blues fan is to understand that the moment something good happens....

Duck!

Good must always be followed by a dark and painful downside. The "Monday Night Miracle" is considered the greatest game in Blues history and one of the more electrifying finishes in St. Louis sports history (see Argument #13). On May 12, 1986, in Game 6 of the Campbell Conference finals, the Blues rallied from a 5–2 deficit in the final 11 minutes, 52 seconds to tie the Flames. Then Doug Wickenheiser scored in overtime to force a Game 7 of the Campbell Conference finals and turn St. Louis into an overjoyed hockey town.

Everyone was going nuts because it seemed inevitable that the Blues would go into Calgary, win the game, and head off to the Stanley Cup finals.

There was only one minor detail everyone overlooked. They had to play the game.

Of course, the Blues lost Game 7, which some wise guys dubbed the "Wednesday Night Reality Check."

Most of the heartbreak was rendered in the postseason. There were 25 straight trips to the playoffs with no Stanley Cup payoff. Perhaps the worst of all was the 1999–2000 Blues team that won the NHL President's Trophy with a

THE BEST ST. LOUIS SPORTS ARGUMENTS

51–20–11–1 record. That team was loaded with talent. Goalie Roman Turek had 42 victories in the nets. Chris Pronger became the first defenseman since Bobby Orr to claim the league MVP (Hart Trophy) and the Norris Trophy as the league's top defenseman.

If only it could have stopped there.

This team looked ready for a long and prosperous run in the Stanley Cup playoffs, yet got knocked out in the first round by the San Jose Sharks.

Another example of bad always following good was the free-agent signing of Scott Stevens in 1990. How did that work out? In the quintessential "it seemed like a good idea at the time" Blues moment, the signing of Stevens resulted in St. Louis giving up five No. 1 picks to Washington as compensation for the defenseman. One year later, on September 3, 1991, the NHL awarded Stevens to the New Jersey Devils in a controversial arbitration case as compensation for the Blues signing free agent Brendan Shanahan from New Jersey.

This is just what the Blues do.

Wayne Gretzky was traded to the Blues with 18 games remaining in the 1995–96 regular season. The "Great One" was being teamed up with Brett Hull and the Blues were on the verge of a dynasty.

Not so fast. The team lost in the playoffs. GM-coach Mike Keenan alienated Gretzky, who then left St. Louis as a free agent and signed with the New York Rangers.

There's more. Shall we go on?

Brett Hull was the first hockey player to come to St. Louis with any genuine star power. He made going to Blues games an important event on the social calendar, recharging the city's interest in hockey with 50 goals in the first 49 games of the 1990–91 season. He was responsible for the explosion of youth hockey in this town.

Of course, the Blues couldn't keep him, and an ugly contract hassle ended with Hull fleeing the city as a free agent in 1998. He went on to win Stanley Cups in Dallas and Detroit.

Nonetheless, as painful as it is to be a Blues fan, it is nothing like being a Cubs fan because Blues fans can always say they've at least been *close* to winning it all once or twice over the last century.

DID THE BLUES MAKE THE RIGHT MOVE IN TRADING BRENDAN SHANAHAN?

76 In the conventional wisdom of the day, when Blues general manager-head coach Mike Keenan traded away Brendan Shanahan to the

Hartford Whalers, it didn't much matter to Blues fans who they were getting in return.

It didn't matter that they were getting a 6-foot-6 young defenseman with unlimited potential named Chris Pronger. All they knew was Shanahan was leaving, and in the fans' minds this was just one more reason to hate Keenan. All they knew was he had just sent the most popular player on the team packing, a man who had been one of the best scorers in team history. During the 1992–93 season, he scored 51 goals and added 43 assists for a total of 94 points. Next season, he scored 102 points (52 goals, 50 assists).

As it turned out, getting Pronger turned out to be more than a fair exchange for Shanahan. In his eight seasons in St. Louis, "Prongs" made five All-Star teams, and won the 2000 Hart Trophy as the NHL MVP. Pronger was the first defenseman in 28 years—after Bobby Orr—to win the league MVP.

And talk about what goes around comes around. When Pronger was traded after the 2004–05 lockout due to the team's inability to meet his contract demands, fans met his departure with some of the same anger they had when Shanahan departed. The Blues fan base was livid about this deal, because they lost (now get this) a fan favorite and All-Star defenseman in exchange for a collection of average players from the Edmonton Oilers (Eric Brewer, Jeff Woywitka, and Doug Lynch).

WHO WAS THE BEST OWNER IN ST. LOUIS BLUES HISTORY?

77 Here's a rather odd situation concerning who was the best owner of the Blues: If Bill Laurie had not lost interest in the team and gotten desperate to dump salaries in order to sell the franchise, he might have been considered the team's greatest owner. Until he put the team on the market in 2006, Laurie did not pinch pennies. He put a quality product on the ice and Blues fans filled the arena every home game.

Years from now, I suspect we'll have to alter this entry and insert new owner Dave Checketts, because I believe he and his top aide John Davidson will fix the mess they were left by Laurie.

For the time being, however, the original owner of the franchise, Sid Salomon, gets my vote.

Salomon and his son, Sid Salomon III, got the expansion franchise in June 1966. The players loved Salomon because he tried to build the team the right way and treated them like family.

At the end of the season, he would take the entire team on a trip to Florida, providing cars for everyone. He put them in The Arena and spent money to renovate the shabby place, with a private dinner club, new seats, paint, and air conditioning. His best move would prove to be the inexpensive hire of his first head coach, Scotty Bowman. It only cost Salomon $15,000 a year to get Bowman, and along with general manager Lynn Patrick, they began to put the team together. They added smart talent like goalies Glenn Hall and Jacques Plante, defenseman Doug Harvey, and forward Dickie Moore, along with Barclay Plager, Noel Picard, and Red Berenson.

"Hockey games became a very important social function," said K T R S radio broadcaster Mike Claiborne, a life-long resident and hockey fan. "We're talking women in fur coats and men in suits and ties. It wasn't like it is today where you find people wearing just about anything to a Blues game. When the team first came to town, man, it was a place to see and be seen. You have to give Sid Salomon Jr. the credit for that."

WHO WAS THE WORST OWNER IN ST. LOUIS BLUES HISTORY?

78 After the Salomons ran into tough times, they sold the team to the St. Louis-based pet food giant Ralston Purina in 1977. That sale ensured that the franchise would not move to Canada. With Ralston Purina running the show, things initially changed for the better. A year after winning a franchise-worst 18 games, the Blues made the playoffs, and began a run of 25 consecutive playoff appearances. The financial woes continued for the franchise, however, and by 1983 Purina claimed to lose an estimated $1.8 million a year. With the retirement of the company's longtime chairman, R. Hal Dean, the company quickly lost interest in ownership of a hockey team.

The Blues were back on the market. In the meantime, the Purina ownership group cut costs by not even sending any representatives to the 1983 draft. That's right, the Blues forfeited their entire draft. Purina abandoned the franchise until it found potential buyers, but that only made a bad situation worse. A group of investors led by Canadian Bill Hunter tried to buy the Blues and planned to move the franchise to Saskatoon, Saskatchewan, until the NHL vetoed the sale and took over temporary ownership.

Why not Harry Ornest? Other than making the terrible mistake of allowing his wife to re-design the Blues uniforms, Ornest's other major crime of ownership was the penny-pinching way he ran the team. He never provided Bernie Federko and Brian Sutter with enough talent to compete for the Stanley Cup on a consistent basis. But the Los Angeles-based businessman saved the franchise from contraction when he agreed to purchase the team, and thus Ralston Purina beats him for our honor here.

ONE GOALIE, ONE GAME:

Who Do You Pick?

Suppose that for one game—and one game only—your life depends on the outcome of a hockey showdown. Which current or former Blues goalie would you pick?

There are plenty of stars to choose from. Glenn Hall, Mike Liut, and Grant Fuhr are among the best to ever guard the net. But with your life on the line, wouldn't you want the innovative net minder, Jacques Plante?

Plante came out of retirement in 1968 to join the Blues for only two seasons. Nonetheless, at the age of 40 he led the

Blues to back-to-back Stanley Cup finals and shared the Vezina Trophy with Hall as the league's most outstanding goalie. When you think of Plante's ability, you have to call him the father of modern goaltending. He popularized the goalie mask, was the first goalie to skate behind the nets to stop the puck for his defensive teammates, and created a hand signal to let teammates know icing had been called. He showed a new generation of goalies about position goaltending, cutting off angles and squaring his body in front of the shooter. He could stand on his head any time, anywhere. He even started as goalie for 502 games in the pre-mask era, a streak that will likely never be broken.

NO HULL, NO GRETZKY:
Who Do You Pick?

The answer is Pierre Turgeon.

Why not Bernie Federko? Federko is a Hall of Famer, a popular member of the Blues as both a player and a broadcaster. He has a bronze statue in front of Scottrade Center, and his sweater hangs from the rafters at Scottrade Center. Turgeon has no statue nor does his sweater hang from the upper reaches of the arena… yet.

So why Turgeon, a man who was only here for four seasons?

For those four seasons, he was the better shooter and skater, a genuine star-power goal scorer (more than 500 career goals) who will end up in the Hall of Fame when he retires. Turgeon was often described as "an artist" by writers and broadcasters who covered the team. In the 1999–2000 season, he scored 66 points in 52 games and helped the team to a franchise-record 115 points and the President's Trophy. A prime example of what he meant to the Blues was a 2001 game against the defending Stanley Cup champion New Jersey Devils. Playing without three of their top-line players—Chris Pronger, Pavol Demitra, and Michal Handzus—the Blues defeated the Devils 4–3 because of Turgeon's artistry on the ice. He scored two goals, including the game winner in overtime that he calmly plucked out of the air with his stick in front of the goal.

WHO IS THE MOST HATED MAN IN ST. LOUIS HOCKEY HISTORY?

81

The answer is Mike Keenan, of course.

Well, why not... are you kidding me? There is no "why not" in this category.

Ask anyone who loves the Blues to say something nice about Mike Keenan, and they'll likely offer this: It sure was nice to see the jerk finally leave.

There are so many reasons why Keenan became one of the most unpopular sports figures in St. Louis history. But the easiest way to settle an argument about why the former Blues coach is so despised is this overwhelming one: He ran the "Great One" out of town.

When the Blues acquired Gretzky from the Los Angeles Kings for forwards Craig Johnson, Patrice Tardif, defenseman Roman Vopat, and a first- and fifth-round pick on February 27, 1996, it was one of the best things to ever happen to St. Louis hockey.

Keenan had swung a deal that would put the world's greatest hockey player on the same ice with his good friend Brett Hull. But the good times did not last. After only 18 regular-season games and a disappointing postseason, Gretzky had enough of the dark and annoying Keenan. Five months later, the "Great One" bolted from St. Louis as a free agent and signed with the New York Rangers. As a result, the Blues were left empty-handed, their fans furious.

Before being fired in December of 1996, Keenan the general manager/coach had tried the patience of everyone who followed the Blues from afar, as well as practically everyone inside the Blues organization.

It began badly enough when he dumped fan favorites Petr Nedved, Craig Janney, and Brendan Shanahan within a year of stepping into the front office. The Shanahan trade in particular outraged Blues fans. It only got worse in July of 1996 when he signed aging right winger Joe Murphy to a three-year, $9.8 million deal that made him the laughing-stock of the entire NHL.

When you lose the greatest hockey player of all time in Gretzky, then try to sell everybody that an old man will replace his scoring power (Murphy scored 24 goals in 102 games), it's easy to see why so many Blues fans turned on Keenan. Somehow, he managed to survive two more seasons after the Gretzky deal didn't pan out, but Keenan finally sealed his doom during the next season when he took the team captaincy away from Hull. His era ended midway through that season, on December 19, 1996, and Blues Nation rejoiced.

TRADITION...
TRADITION

ST. LOUIS' BEST (AND WORST) SPORTS TRADITIONS

This all-inclusive category covers every sports tradition in St. Louis that we could think of, both great and not-so-great, exalted and questionable, memorable and regrettable. What we're trying to do is wander into some sacred territory, exploring every aspect of the best and worst of St. Louis' sports customs. As we go about the business of exploring these traditions, nothing, you will see, is taboo.

TELL THE TRUTH:

Doesn't Stan "The Man" Deserve a Better Statue?

82
"Here stands baseball's perfect warrior."
"Here stands baseball's perfect knight."
　　Those famous words from former baseball commissioner Ford Frick are inscribed on the base of the famous Stan Musial statue outside Busch Stadium. The words are wonderful, but let's be perfectly honest: They don't belong on this statue. I am about to mention one of the greatest sports taboos in St. Louis. It's a subject everyone thinks about, but no one dares speak.

The legendary Stan Musial statue isn't very good.

Okay, let me tell you what I really think.

I think it stinks.

I think it's ugly.

I think it's grossly out of proportion. The hat looks goofy. The elegant Musial looks like a thick and beefy longshoreman. When they put it in storage after the demolition of the old stadium, I was praying some clumsy worker lost his grip on the crane and the whole thing broke into a hundred little bronze pieces that the Cardinals could have auctioned off to fans for a thousand dollars.

The truth is, Musial never really liked his famous statue either. He told the *St. Louis Post-Dispatch* in 2004 that the sculptor, former Washington University fine arts professor Carl Mose, "made me all bulky. I tried to get him to change it, but he just never would. So finally I told him, 'Well, just go on and get it done.' He never did get it right."

Stan "The Man" preferred another design—the decidedly more artistic and authentic one crafted by local sculptor Harry Weber, which currently resides at the Missouri Sports Hall of Fame in Springfield. Another model also sits in front of a suburban St. Louis restaurant.

I'm with Stan "The Man." If you put the Weber statue next to the Mose statue, you'd think one was done by a professional sculptor and one by a young art student. Musial loved the Weber statue not only because it was the original design, but also because Weber brought the greatest living Cardinal to his studio and got his opinion. After instituting several changes that Musial requested, Weber completed the work with Musial's blessing.

So if Musial loved the Weber statue so much, how did we end up with the odd looking Mose design?

As the story goes, back in the 1960s, Missouri sportswriters began fund-raising efforts to pay for a statue based on the 1963 rendering by former *Post-Dispatch* artist Amadee Wohlschlager called "The Boy and The Man...Baseball's Bond." Amadee's drawing showed Musial signing an autograph for a smiling young boy. But the fund drive fell $40,000 short, and the Amadee model was ditched by then-St. Louis mayor Raymond Tucker, who instead gave the project to his friend Mose.

As a result, since 1968 we've been stuck with the ugly statue that is supposed to be a dead ringer for Musial in his famous batting stance, but is just an out-of-proportion odd-looking mess by Professor Mose instead of the cool one sculpted by the gifted Weber. It's funny and rather curious why the Cards haven't gotten the Weber, since all the other bronze statues that honor their Hall of Fame heroes are fine pieces of art crafted by Weber.

Maybe they're just afraid to rock the boat. Maybe they just need a little guidance. Maybe they need to know that we think it's an ugly statue, too.

IS ST. LOUIS REALLY A GREAT BASEBALL TOWN?

83 Several years ago, as I stood on the top steps of the visitors' dugout in old Busch Stadium, leaning on the railing and chatting with former San Francisco Giants manager Dusty Baker, we watched the fans begin to stream into the ballpark.

I was visiting St. Louis at the time, on an assignment in my old job as a correspondent for HBO's *Real Sports*. The game was still several hours away, but already the place was filling up with red-clad devotees of Cardinals Nation. As Baker watched the pilgrims file in, he smiled.

"This is the best baseball town in America," he told me. "These folks love their team and know the game."

I listened carefully as Baker looked out at the stadium and pointed out everything he loved about St. Louis the baseball town. He pointed to the old-fashioned green scoreboard in the center field upper deck. He motioned to the stands, where all the fans in their Cardinals jerseys, T-shirts, polos, and throwbacks clutched their scorecards and politely beckoned the players to *"Pul-eeeez..."* sign an autograph.

A few years later, across the other side of the field, I had a similar conversation with Cardinals manager Tony La Russa, who tried to explain to me—a newcomer to the city—what made the Redbirds fan different from all the other sports fans in other cities.

"It's not really their knowledge of the game that makes them special," La Russa told me. "It's their passion. They do not boo performance. They boo effort. You can make a bad play, you can strike out, you can have a bad night at the plate or on the mound. They understand that. What they don't understand is a guy who ain't trying. If they think you're not trying, they'll boo you as hard as any place in America."

So now that I've lived here more than five years and have carefully observed the habits of the local fanatics, I can say with no hesitation that I see that passion La Russa and Baker were describing. I watch Cardinals fans stream into Busch Stadium at the rate of more than three million spectators a season (eight of nine years from 1998 through 2006). I see them turn the streets of downtown St. Louis into a college sports town on so many summer days and nights whenever the Cards are in town.

I see them sell out game after game after game.

But over the past few years, I have also seen some things that La Russa and Baker didn't tell me about.

When I see the ballpark filled to the brim at the start of every home game with more than 43,000 spectators, I am impressed. When I see a sea of red and white in those seats every night, I am impressed. St. Louis fans support their baseball team like major university football fans support their teams.

But then I see the weeknight game edging toward the sixth inning, with the result not close to being resolved, and I see 10,000 empty seats or more. I look outside and I see cars flowing toward the highway, and suddenly I have a vision of an entirely different sort of fan base.

I think of the Los Angeles sports fan, that indifferent, traffic jam-conscious species of Dodgers fan who is more concerned with making good time on the local expressways than whether or not the local team is going to win or lose.

Then I stroll around the ballpark on a hot summer afternoon, and I listen to the sounds of these "greatest baseball fans" and I hear something that sounds like it comes from the bleachers in Philadelphia or the Bronx. This "great" baseball town is developing a mean streak and a reflex of impatience and intolerance. I hear them boo performance now. I listen to a growing segment of Cardinals Nation act like drunken bores as they sit in the bleachers, tossing back brews and cursing out players who aren't as good as they want them to be.

During the 2006 championship season, when I heard some of the nastiest, mean-spirited boos coming from the stands, and the most heartless impatience on radio talk shows, I reminded La Russa of his comment about when and why Cardinals fans boo players.

"I thought you told me Cards fans don't boo perform-ance," I said.

"Well actually what I think I said was they *rarely* boo

performance," La Russa said with a sly chuckle. "But when properly motivated, they'll boo you just as bad as the worst fan from Philadelphia. They're not perfect. But they're as close as you're going to get."

I will admit that St. Louis has the *appearance* of a great baseball town, particularly over the last decade when the Cardinals have been so successful on the field. Since 1998 when they began their run of drawing three million-plus fans, there has usually been a good reason why the team's loyalists have made their pilgrimages to Busch. It began with the Mark McGwire home run chase in 1998, and was followed up with a string of six first-place finishes in seven seasons and two trips to the World Series over a three-year period.

But does that mean that St. Louis *is* a great baseball town, or just an involved sports town that truly rallies around winners?

Put an above-average product in front of St. Louis fans, and they respond. If you look at attendance patterns in St. Louis, most of the upward and downward surges hinge on the on-field (or on-ice) success or failure of the local teams. When the Rams were the Greatest Show on Turf, you couldn't get a ticket in town. But last year, after two consecutive 8–8 seasons, the sellouts came to an end. For the first time since moving into the Dome, they did not sell out a home game.

When the Blues started losing, the fans abandoned them, too. When the St. Louis U basketball team plays a nationally ranked team, they draw 16,000 to 19,000 fans. When they play a run-of-the-mill team, they barely draw 5,000 spectators. As the Missouri Valley Conference's national profile surged, so did its tournament's attendance figures.

So if you trace attendance at Cardinals games over the decades, the turnstiles tell the truth. In the non-competitive 1970s when the team never finished higher than second in their division, the team didn't draw more than 1.7 million fans a season. In the 1980s with the arrival of Whitey Herzog and four first-place finishes, attendance rose to over two million a season. Attendance peaked at a club-record 3.08 million spectators in 1989, but went on a steady decline in the early 1990s when manager Joe Torre couldn't get the team to finish any higher than second in the division.

Attendance bottomed out to below two million during the strike-shortened 1994 and 1995 losing seasons, but once La Russa came in and started winning division titles the turnstiles started turning again.

So my gut tells me that even though baseball is a part of the Midwestern cultural fabric, if this ball club starts losing again, the fans will show the same disinterest they showed with the Rams and Blues.

The real truth is that St. Louis might really care about baseball, but what they really love more than anything else is winning. In recent history, the Cardinals have all the other teams in St. Louis beat in that most critical statistic.

IS ST. LOUIS THE CRADLE OF THE GREATEST SPORTS ANNOUNCERS?

84 For obvious reasons, New York has produced more than its fair share of legendary broadcast voices in sports radio and television. So let's give it credit for the impressive number of great sports announcers who earned their fame or spent part of their careers behind the microphone in the Big Apple.

Yet for a mid-sized sports town, St. Louis has been an outstanding proving ground to many significant broadcast voices who spent time here honing their crafts.

From Jack Buck to Harry Caray, Bob Costas to Joe Buck, and all the Jay Randolphs, Dan Dierdorfs, Mike Shannons, and Joe Garagiolas in between, St. Louis has played a major role in grooming an abundance of legendary broadcast voices. While New York understandably has the most former radio/TV broadcasters in the Baseball Hall of Fame broadcasters wing (five), St. Louis ranks right behind with three: Buck, Caray, and Garagiola.

For the answer to why so many outstanding voices have worked in St. Louis, the mystery begins and ends with four letters:

K-M-O-X.

Those famous call letters represent the powerful radio station that began the concept of talk radio. KMOX was the training ground for generations of outstanding broadcasters, beginning with the smooth and conventional Jack Buck and his hilarious and unconventional sidekick, Harry Caray. Buck spent nearly his entire career inside the KMOX booth, and by the time of his death at age 77 in 2002 he was clearly identified as the ultimate face and voice of Cardinals baseball.

If not for an alleged bit of hanky-panky, the face and voice could have been—and probably should have been—a two-headed symbol. Harry Caray, born Harry Christopher Carabina in St. Louis on March 1, 1914, began his broadcasting career in 1945 on KMOX doing Cardinals games. Possibly more important, he was also the charismatic on-air salesman for the team's chief sponsor, Busch beer. There's no telling how long Caray could have remained in the KMOX booth if he had not run afoul of team owner August Busch in 1969. Busch fired Caray; to this day the urban legend is that it was as a result of an alleged affair Caray had with the owner's daughter-in-law.

The powerful signal of KMOX was the lure that attracted many young broadcasters and retired athletes to the booth in St. Louis. And while it's hard to imagine listening to some of the shrill nonsense that passes for sports talk radio in town today, KMOX perfected the medium of sports talk with intelligent and witty conversations long before the rest of the nation caught on to the phenomenon.

And that's why St. Louis deserves to be recognized as the cradle of sports announcers.

WHY AREN'T THERE ANY COMMEMORATIVE STATUES OUTSIDE THE EDWARD JONES DOME?

85 As any long-time St. Louis sports fan knows and every transplant quickly discovers, St. Louis politics can ruin any good idea in short order. Politics—city politics in particular—rarely operate on the same rational ground rules that control the sports world. The end game in this convoluted environment is determined by rules only Kafka or a faceless bureaucrat would understand. Right is wrong. Bad is good. Nonsense is preferred over the rational.

I first discovered this five years ago, not long after I arrived in St. Louis and wondered aloud why the Rams football stadium—the Edward Jones Dome—did not have the same impressive statue plaza outside its walls that decorates the baseball Cardinals' home down the street on

Broadway. Busch Stadium is well known for the plaza of statues of the city's greatest Hall of Fame baseball heroes—Stan Musial, Bob Gibson, Lou Brock, Red Schoendienst, and all the others.

"Everyone always knows when you're going to a Cardinal game, you can tell someone 'Hey, meet me at the Stan Musial statue,'" says Bill Mathis, president of Mathis-Jones Communications and Sports Archives. "But when you go to a Rams game, there's nothing around the Dome that symbolizes any of this city's pro football past. You go to a Rams game and you say 'Meet me ... uhhh ... where?'"

Mathis and a committee of local business types tried in vain to change that situation five years ago with "The Handoff?"—a twice-life-sized figure showing Kurt Warner appear to hand the ball off to Marshall Faulk during the Rams' 1999 Super Bowl season. While Warner and Faulk were the subjects of the statue, Mathis said his committee's plan called for the names of "every player, every person, every administrative individual who was part of the magic that led the Rams' Super Bowl season" to be engraved around the base of the statue.

The entire project would have been financed privately from the proceeds of the sale of 50 miniature bronze replicas of "The Handoff?" (price tag for the 18-inch replicas: $10,000 each). It would not cost the city a dime. This was the ultimate great idea.

Yet here we are five years later, and the project has met

with hard resistance from the St. Louis Regional Convention and Sports Complex Authority, which operates the Edward Jones Dome for the city, county, and state. Five years ago, the head of the authority, Renee Kleffner, complained to Mathis that she didn't know why Warner and Faulk were featured. She worried Warner could be traded. She said the statue should have been of Mike Jones' famous goal-line tackle that preserved the Rams' Super Bowl victory.

Then the commission haggled over the location of the statue.

What I learned from most long-time St. Louis natives is that if you understand city politics you would understand why the project never gained traction. No matter how great the idea was, the biggest problem that the folks at the authority had with "The Handoff?" was that they didn't think of it themselves.

"The Handoff?" should have been just the beginning of a series of football statues lining the streets around the Dome. Why aren't there bronze tributes to the former Cardinals football greats of the past outside the Dome? Why don't we have bronze statues of the great Rams of the past out there? The Los Angeles history of the Rams came with the team the minute the franchise moved to St. Louis, but it seems to have gotten lost on the trip. There is no other place to honor the greats like Deacon Jones, Merlin Olsen, Dick (Night Train) Lane, Bob Waterfield, Crazylegs

Hirsch, Eric Dickerson, Jack Youngblood, and all the other L.A. Rams Hall of Famers.

If you go to the football Cardinals' new stadium in Arizona, you can see large displays and murals in their corridors regarding the St. Louis history of the franchise.

If the sorriest organization in football can figure that out, why can't the Rams?

OLD BUSCH VS. NEW BUSCH:

Which Ballpark Is the Best?

86 Come on. Do we really have to engage in this debate?

This is like asking someone if he prefers that baby blue polyester leisure suit from the 1970s to a super 200 blue wool pinstripe that was custom-tailored for him last week.

Unless you are a freak for really tacky retro, there's no way you can choose old Busch over new Busch.

Well what about those marvelous arches on the old stadium roof that cast those cool shadows over the field?

Glad you brought that up. It's the single redeeming architectural aspect of that concrete monstrosity that was part of the cookie-cutter, multi-purpose stadium craze of the 1960s and 1970s. Everything else about old Busch, like the artificial turf that turned the playing surface into a scorching griddle on any typical summer day, was an aesthetic eyesore.

Even when the Cardinals organization tried to doll it up with natural grass, the old green scoreboard, and the retired numbers in the outfield upper deck, it was like putting lipstick on a pig. To truly understand why old Busch was so bad, you had to take a stroll through the bowels of Busch, where rusty water dripped through wall crevices, and odd, inexplicable sounds echoed off the walls.

During the final season in old Busch, reporters used to crowd into manager Tony La Russa's office for his daily pregame chat, and without fail a weird, rattling, grinding, whining sound used to emanate from the ceiling in his bathroom.

"Somebody turn on your tape recorder and play that noise any time somebody complains about tearing this place down," La Russa used to joke.

The new Busch Stadium is one of the best new ballparks in baseball because it does not try to overwhelm you with gimmicks and gadgets. Its beauty is in its simplicity. It is a charming brick structure with subtle charms like the brownstone cardinal plaques that dot the infield walls. It doesn't feel like an amusement park with trains on the outfield wall, waterfalls or hot tubs in the bleachers, or oversized stone tigers lurking on the exterior façade.

New Busch is not without its modern touches or even a few modern complaints. Some old-schoolers complain that the best seats have been reserved for the high rollers and the high prices of food and drink have made it difficult for a family to afford to come to the games. But that's the high cost of doing business in modern professional sports.

New Busch has done a good job of balancing the old with the new. So if your culinary stadium tastes are satisfied by a brat and a brew, or cotton candy and a tall cup of soda, they can give you that.

But if you want gourmet pizza, stir-fry Chinese food, sliced meats and cheeses, a hunk of expensive cheesecake, chocolate-covered strawberries, or a fancy cup of overpriced coffee, and you want to eat all of this while dining in an air-conditioned club level with flat-screen TVs all around, new Busch has provided that luxury, too.

Yet the most important attraction of new Busch Stadium is that once you enter the gates, it gets out of the way and lets you see the baseball game without any goofy distractions. The inside of the ballpark has been set up to give everyone great sightlines for great views of the field. There is an intimacy to this place with bleachers surrounding the bullpens and the low walls in the infield. Take a stroll around the upper decks and you will find standing-room vantage points that might be as good as any seat in the place.

New Busch is a classic. Old Busch was just old.

WHAT'S THE BEST ST. LOUIS SPORTS MOVIE?

87 There are many good and not-so-good sports movies with direct and indirect St. Louis connections: *The Pride of St. Louis* (1952), *The Game of Their Lives* (2005), *BASEketball* (1998 comedy with Bob Costas in a cameo role), and the 2005 remake of *The Longest Yard* (with St. Louis rap star Nelly in a starring role and me—yes, me—in a riveting cameo performance as a sports writer).

While we will long remember the Oscar-worthy performance of Costas doing the play-by-play in the Denslow Cup championship series, *BASEketball*, for all its satirical splendor, cannot be considered as a St. Louis movie just because one guy from the 'Lou is yukking it up on camera.

And while two St. Louis guys in a movie might be slightly better than one, *The Longest Yard* is about a bunch of convict football players in a Texas state prison. Again, that's not enough of a strong St. Louis tie (though to this day I do not understand how I was not nominated for an Academy Award for my brilliant delivery of my one line, "Awww man!!"). Of course, to this day I maintain that it was by far the best Hollywood movie I've ever been in.

So that leaves us with the two "reel" St. Louis sports flicks, full of local connections: *The Game of Their Lives*, the story of the U.S. soccer team's amazing upset of England in the 1950 World Cup, and *The Pride of St. Louis*, a 1952 film biography of former Cardinals Hall of Fame pitcher Dizzy Dean.

The Game is a more serious flick with stronger St. Louis connections. In 1950, the United States received an invitation to compete in the World Cup in Brazil. Faced with budget constraints, the United States decided to go to the country's biggest soccer hotbed, St. Louis, to recruit a group of local players who had no professional or international experience. It tells the story of St. Louis natives Frank Borghi, Harry Keough, Gino Pariani, Frank "Pee Wee" Wallace, and Charles "Gloves" Columbo, as well as Haitian-born New Yorker Joe Gatjeans and Philadelphian Walter Bahr.

The Game of Their Lives shot most of its pre-Brazil scenes in St. Louis, and recruited many of the extras from the community. It's a touching movie, although its familiar sports movie themes tend to make it rather predictable.

In *The Pride of St. Louis*, Dan Dailey plays Dizzy Dean and Richard Crenna plays his brother Paul (Daffy) Dean. If you love classic baseball movies, this is a DVD that you immediately need to add to your collection. Having Dailey in the role of Dizzy Dean is good for any number of reasons. He adds the perfect, aw-shucks comic touch. Better yet, he throws the ball like an athlete. Too often in

215

those old sports-related movies, the actors playing the sports figures are horrible athletes.

Here's what makes *Pride* better than *The Game*: It's fun. We know it's over-the-top and slightly inaccurate in some of the portrayals of Dean's life. But Dan Dailey pulls this performance off well, emphasizing Dean's corny 1930s dialogue and his ability to capture the boastful country boy with his fractured vocabulary.

WHAT IS THE BEST NICKNAME IN ST. LOUIS SPORTS HISTORY?

88 This is one of the toughest arguments in the book. I've waded through countless research and discovered some of the best and most colorful nicknames in sports seem to have emanated from St. Louis: "Easy Ed" Macauley, Torry "Big Game" Holt, "The Donut Boys" (Adam Timmerman and Andy McCollum), Leo "The Lip" Durocher, Cliff "Lil' Abner" Hagan, Pepper "The Wild Horse of the Osage" Martin, Joe "Ducky" Medwick, Enos "Country" Slaughter, Steven "Train" Jackson, Al "The Mad Hungarian" Hrabrosky. I love them all, but ultimately I narrowed down my list to this Magnificent Seven, based largely on originality, style, and timelessness. I promise you'll be surprised—and entertained—by my unexpected No. 1.

7. BIG BLUE:

Maybe I was just looking for a way to get the legendary St. Louis Hawks radio play-by-play man Buddy Blattner mentioned in the book, but he gets the credit for this moniker given to the great Bob Pettit. Blattner says he gave Pettit the nickname shortly after he arrived in St. Louis in the 1950s because during the winter the 6-foot-9 power forward would wear an ugly, long blue overcoat that made him look "like the front wall of a blue handball court."

6. EL HOMBRE:

This clever Latin spinoff of Stan "The Man" was given to Albert Pujols several years ago, to the best of my recollection, by *St. Louis Post-Dispatch* colleague Bernie Miklasz. Some old-schoolers hate the nickname because they say it disrespects Musial's nickname and status as the ultimate Cardinal. But I give style points to Miklasz for using the Spanish translation to dub the only other Cardinals hitter who could ever even hope to end up on the same plateau with Musial.

5. THE WIZARD OF OZ:

Ozzie Smith was so cool, so stylish, so athletic that he needed a handle that perfectly captured his GQ essence.

217

"The Wizard of Oz" and its shorter, hipper "The Wiz" fit him as well as one of his expensive tailor-made suits.

4. STAN "THE MAN":

Brooklyn Dodgers fans gave Musial his famous nickname, and it seemed to be an ideal fit: simplistic and understated, yet direct and to the point. Some nicknames end up passing down through the athletic generations (Sugar Ray), but no other Stanleys have been able to measure up to Musial in more than a half century, which tells you just how remarkable he was and how special his nickname proved to be.

3. DIZZY AND DAFFY:

Well now, how can you separate the Dean boys and their comical and clever nicknames? Dizzy (Jay Hanna) and Daffy (Paul) Dean will always go in as a single entry in the nickname book of records. We're really not sure why Jay Hanna ended up with the nickname "Dizzy." We only know that his Army sergeant gave it to him. But it was a perfect fit, as the iconoclast proved to be one of the most flamboyant showmen in baseball.

2. COOL PAPA:

Under most normal circumstances, it would be hard *not to* pick a nickname like "Cool Papa" as the best moniker going. "Cool Papa" Bell was a Hall of Famer as a baseball player and in the nickname game, too. The Negro Leagues produced some of the most imaginative nicknames in the history of sports. So if I loved this one so much, why did I rank it No. 2? How could I not after what I'm about to explain to you now…

1. THE BIG SWEAT:

Who???? There's a good reason you're not familiar with this nickname. Not too many people outside of the inner circle of former Rams know about this one. Remember John St. Clair, the third-round pick out of Virginia in the 2000 draft? St. Clair was a center who spent three seasons with the Rams, mostly as an offensive tackle. So how'd he get the nickname "The Big Sweat"? Well, for the same reason he ended up as a tackle, not a center. According to Mike Martz, when St. Clair came to the Rams he used to sweat profusely, always leaving his uniform soaked to the bone. Most unusually, though, the biggest sweaty buildup was in his butt. "If you saw his gray practice pants, they were always soaking wet," Martz once told me. "The quarterbacks used to hate… well… putting their hands on him when St. Clair was playing center. They'd come away with the ball and a sweat-soaked hand. It was really kind of nasty."

And a legend was born. Guys started calling him "The Big Sweat," and pretty soon, a position change was in order. And I can't think of another nickname that deserves to be ranked No. 1 more than "The Big Sweat."

219

IF YOU COULD HAVE A TICKET TO ANY GAME/EVENT IN ST. LOUIS SPORTS HISTORY, WHAT WOULD IT BE?

89

Allow yourself the fantasy of time travel. You have one golden ticket that will transport you back in time to one eventful moment in St. Louis sports history, allowing you a front-row seat to the biggest game or most historic moment in time.

What would you choose?

Would it be an opportunity to rewind a favorite childhood memory, but this time through more mature eyes? Or would you be more interested in viewing a defining moment in sports history, one that most likely could never be repeated?

If you hit the historic rewind button on St. Louis sports, you'll find plenty to choose from. There is the Rams' exciting run to a Super Bowl title, or maybe it's a second glance at the Cardinals' World Series victory in 1982. Would you love to be in that smoke-filled Kiel Auditorium in 1958 when Bob Pettit scored 50 points to lead the Hawks to their only NBA title? Or how about witnessing Bob Gibson's 17-strikeout shutout of the Detroit Tigers in Game 1 of the 1968 World Series?

But think about this for a moment. How hard would it be to gain access to videotapes of those events? Through the miracle of classic sports collections, many of those events have been captured on tape, film, VHS, and DVD. As a result, I can pop in a DVD of nearly every Cardinals World Series going back to the 1960s. I have seen the Super Bowl victory on ESPN Classic and the NFL Channel every year during Super Bowl week.

So to me, the golden ticket back in time needs to be for some special event that I could not have possibly witnessed before. To me, that leaves only two possible choices: the 1904 Summer Olympics or Jackie Robinson's first game in St. Louis in 1947.

The modern Olympic Games were revived in 1896 in Athens, then moved to Paris in 1900. So by the time they arrived in St. Louis in 1904, it marked the first time the Olympic Games were held on American soil. Oddly enough, the Olympics were not the major international event between nations that they are today. According to the official Olympic organization history, of the 94 events in the 1904 Olympic Games, only 42 athletes were not from the United States.

The majority of the events were held on the campus of Washington University, including the start and finish of the marathon, which was initially won by American Fred Lorz. But when officials were told that Lorz was spotted riding in a car for part of the 42-kilometer race after he got leg cramps, the Gold Medal was awarded to fellow country-man Thomas Hicks. I would have loved to have witnessed that, along with the one-legged American gymnast George Eyser, who won six medals competing with a wooden leg.

Okay, so maybe this is not the ticket I imagined it might be.

So from a historical standpoint, the trip back in time to May 21, 1947, would be worth it just to be among the crowd sitting in the right-field bleachers. That was the "colored" section of old Sportsman's Park, and according to the *St. Louis Post–Dispatch*, at least 6,000 of the 16,249 were black fans crowding into the right-field pavilion, all of them there to cheer on Jackie Robinson and witness firsthand "The Great Experiment."

The game had been postponed from the previous day because of rain storms, but on the morning of May 21 the skies had cleared. As game time neared, on the corner of Grand and Dodier, fans of every color began arriving outside Sportsman's Park, waiting for the gates to open. The crowd was the largest mid-week crowd of the season for the Redbirds. As one witness to the game, Martin Matthews, remembered, the atmosphere was unique to Sportsman's Park. "The [black fans] were all very well dressed," said Matthews, who was a 20-year-old at the time and among the crowd in the pavilion. "Shirts and ties, dresses, all very fancy like we were going to church. It was something to see. Everyone wanted to see Jackie. Everyone wanted to see a black man on the field playing in the major leagues."

Blacks in St. Louis and all over America had more than casual curiosity about "The Great Experiment." They understood that this profound social revolution was not just about baseball. There was far-reaching impact at play here; this was about how well America could tolerate the uncomfortable truth that Robinson was the first wave of many more to come, not just in baseball, but in every aspect of American life.

St. Louis in the 1940s was very much a town with Jim Crow sensibilities more in line with cities in the Deep South than the more racially tolerant northern metropolises. It was considered a "border town" because nearly every aspect of the city's society was segregated. That segregation even extended to Sportsman's Park, where until the 1943 season the Cardinals organization prohibited black patrons from buying tickets in the ballpark's grandstand seats.

In the top of the first inning, Robinson drew a walk from starting pitcher Harry "The Cat" Brecheen, then advanced to third on a single by Pete Reiser. The next batter, Carl Furillo, hit a grounder to first, where Stan Musial scooped it up and stepped on the bag for the first out. Musial instinctively glanced at Robinson, who did not make a break for the plate. So the Cardinals first baseman threw the ball to

223

second trying to double up Reiser. But it was a low wide throw, and as soon as the ball went to second, the fleet-footed Robinson dashed home for the first run of the game.

Robinson would go 0-for-4 in a 10-inning contest, but his first-inning base running helped give the Dodgers a 4–3 victory. *Post-Dispatch* sports editor J. Roy Stockton wrote that, "Robinson was cheered each time he went to bat and the Dodgers as a team received more vocal encouragement than they usually get at Sportsman's Park."

What Stockton didn't write about that "encouragement" was that it was coming from those 6,000 black fans out in the right-field pavilion. "It was quite an event," Matthews remembered. "We were all Cardinal fans, but when Jackie and the Dodgers came to town, we cheered for everything Jackie did. When he came out of the dugout, we cheered. When he came to the plate, we cheered. When he walked, we cheered. If he struck out, it didn't matter much, because we still clapped for him then, too."

If I had been there, I would have been clapping for him, too. A golden ticket into another time and another place, and being in the midst of that bit of St. Louis history, would be hard to match.

SHOULD ST. LOUIS HAVE AN NBA FRANCHISE?

At the present time, St. Louis passionately supports its baseball team and sells out every NFL game, but it is rather ambivalent about its struggling NHL franchise and its one Division I college basketball team.

Is there room for one more team on the St. Louis sports menu?

The St. Louis Hawks left town for Atlanta after the 1968 season, in large part because of the arrival of the expansion NHL team, the Blues. The city's sports fan base made a choice, and in the late 1960s, the preference was hockey over basketball.

Granted, the Hawks were a tremendous financial drain on owner Ben Kerner. However, the underlying reason for the team's failure in St. Louis in the late 1950s and early 1960s was racism, according to author Greg Marecek.

In his book *Full Court: The Untold Stories of the St. Louis Hawks*, Marecek mentioned how Bob Burnes of the *St. Louis Globe-Democrat* wrote a column about the public complaints of Kerner having "too many Negro players" on his team. Marecek wrote how the team got hate mail about the black players, including letters that said, "Why don't you just change your name to the Globetrotters," and another one that said, "We're not coming anymore to watch all those black players."

It's been 40 years since the Hawks left, and times and attitudes in St. Louis have obviously changed since those bad old days.

But have they changed so much that St. Louis deserves one more crack at having an NBA franchise?

I am a long-time, die-hard pro basketball freak, the original Basketball Jones. I am not one of these folks that believes just because the NBA didn't work in St. Louis 40 years ago it can't work today. Times are different, attitudes are different. The area has a larger transient population of residents who grew up in pro basketball cities in the East and West and would grab front-row seats to the Scottrade Center in a heartbeat, which would likely siphon off business from the Blues hockey ticket sales.

This, of course, is the biggest fear of the die-hard hockey fans—all 15,000 of them—in the city. They worried constantly that the old Blues owner Bill Laurie, a former college basketball player, would abandon the hockey team in favor of his real passion, the NBA. It never happened, but now there is that same concern with new Blues owner Dave Checketts, a former NBA executive with the Utah Jazz and New York Knicks. Unlike Laurie, Checketts has friends in the NBA executive suites. If he ever decided to make a play for a hoop franchise, he would likely get it.

But I don't think that happens any time soon, and here's

why. According to NBA executives that I've talked to, the league doesn't believe St. Louis has enough corporate financing to support four pro franchises. One owner told me that while he was sure the team would be able to attract 15,000 to 18,000 spectators a night, the shortcomings of corporate sponsorship would eventually doom the franchise.

"I'm not even convinced St. Louis can afford, at least from a corporate sponsorship standpoint, three pro teams," said the owner (who asked to remain anonymous). "After local companies spend their money and buy their season-ticket packages for the Cardinals and Rams— teams that basically play in different times of the year—if they have any money left over, can they afford to spend it on two winter-schedule teams? Most NBA owners don't think so. They're not even convinced based on the troubles the Blues have experienced, that those companies are willing or able to dish out money for three teams."

Now bring into the mix the rising popularity of the St. Louis U's basketball team, with high-profile coach Rick Majerus sure to bring more corporate interest in the Billikens program.

As a basketball lover who is largely ambivalent about hockey, I love the idea of the "what goes around, comes around" karma of St. Louis bringing in a pro basketball franchise and that team causing an adverse business effect on the hockey team.

227

When you add all this up, St. Louis might deserve an NBA team, but the only way they get it is if the NHL team is no longer here, and that's not going to happen.

WHO'S NEXT? WHO WILL BE THE NEXT GENERATION OF ST. LOUIS SPORTS LEGENDS?

91

5. JOHN DAVIDSON:

The general manager of the St. Louis Blues could end up being one of the most popular men in town if he can return this franchise to the upper echelon of the National Hockey League. When he took over the Blues in 2006, Davidson thought it would be simple to get people to return to the arena and sell out every night. This was, after all, one of the better hockey towns in the United States, and had been for decades. But the one-year labor layoff, coupled with former owner Bill Laurie stripping the club down to bare bones in order to sell it off, alienated almost the entire hockey-loving population. So the fans have been slow to come back. The wounds are deep and painful, and Davidson underestimated how angry hockey lovers were. But he's persistent and convinced that he can make the team competitive quickly and a championship contender in short order. I think he will do it. When that happens, John Davidson will be a local hero.

4. YADIER MOLINA:

There is All-Star potential for the young Cardinals catcher. We already know how good he is as a defensive catcher, because even the running ball clubs tend to respect him and dial back the aggressive base stealing when Molina is behind the plate. But watch his star rise in St. Louis as his batting average improves and he becomes more comfortable with being in the spotlight. Molina has a great personality that is just waiting to come out as he gets more accustomed to speaking English in front of the television cameras. Along with Albert Pujols, he will be one of the cornerstones of the Cardinals future.

3. MIKE ANDERSON:

With the exciting style of play Anderson coaches, he can make Mizzou's basketball team into a Top 25 program again. As soon as he brings in a full complement of players who can execute his "40 Minutes of Hell" attack, a ticket to a Tigers home game will once again be a hot commodity. (In his first year in Columbia in 2006, the Tigers could only play about 15 minutes of hell, about 10 minutes of heck, and the rest of the time, it was "what the heck.") His country charm ought to be appealing to folks in Missouri

229

and an up-tempo calling card should lure some of the best talent in St. Louis to Columbia again.

2. RICK MAJERUS:

The only man who can stop the pipeline from St. Louis to Columbia is Majerus, the colorful new basketball coach at St. Louis University. Majerus has the public persona and nationally recognized coaching résumé that will bring people flocking to Billiken games again. In his first few months on the job, he already began collecting local recruits. Don't be surprised to see SLU basketball games become a tough ticket to land in the very near future.

1. STEVEN JACKSON:

No one in the St. Louis market has as much upside star potential as the Rams running back with the flowing dreadlocks and powerful running style. In 2006, Jackson had a breakthrough season, rushing for 1,528 yards and 13 touchdowns. He also led all running backs when he caught 90 passes for 806 yards, in addition to three touchdowns. He also led the NFL in total yards from scrimmage with 2,334 and was named to the Pro Bowl for the first time in his three-year career. But there's more to his star quality than his play.

There is a lot of showman in his 6-foot-2, 235-pound body, which is to be expected of a kid who grew up in the shadows of the gaudy Las Vegas strip.

Maybe all that long-term exposure to the Vegas glitz has that effect on you. You spend all your life watching headliners, and you figure out exactly how to behave once the spotlight finds you.

Check him out after a game when he makes sure to be fully dressed before meeting with the press. What you get is the full effect: He is the hippest of hipsters with his finely tailored suits, custom-made dress shirts, perfectly knotted silk ties, flowing dreadlocks, and ultra-cool wrap-around sunglasses. When he first arrived in St. Louis, it was easy to believe that he was all style and little substance. Now we know better. He is a hard-working team leader who is obsessed with being great, leading his team to championships and wiping Marshall Faulk's name out of the Rams record book. These are all lofty goals, but don't be surprised if he accomplishes them all.

WHAT WAS THE GREATEST INDIVIDUAL BASKETBALL PERFORMANCE IN ST. LOUIS SPORTS HISTORY?

92 There are only two possible choices for this question, and they will provoke endless debate. Both were done in championship environments, with two superstars producing uncanny memorable shows. So how do you decide between Bill Walton's near-perfection in the 1973 NCAA national championship game and Bob Pettit's 50-point game that led the St. Louis Hawks to the 1958 NBA title?

This is not going to be easy.

Let's begin with Walton's game, which arguably was the best individual performance in NCAA Final Four history. In an 87–66 victory over Memphis State in the 1973 Final Four in St. Louis at the old Checkerdome, Walton made 21 of 22 field goals, scored 44 points, and collected 13 rebounds to lead UCLA to college basketball's national championship. It's hard to imagine a better performance by any college athlete under any circumstances.

But how does it measure up to the greatest individual performance by a professional?

The date was Saturday, April 12, 1958. The backdrop was Game 6 of the NBA finals. The St. Louis Hawks held a 3–2 lead in the best-of-seven championship series over the defending champion Boston Celtics. Pettit scored a then NBA finals-record 50 points to lead the Hawks to a Game 6 victory and the NBA title.

Let's break down the two games:

THE SETUP:

The 1957–58 season was one of many Hall of Fame type seasons for Pettit. He averaged 24.6 points and 17.4 rebounds to lead the Hawks to the Western Division crown with a 41–31 record. The Hawks would face the powerful Boston Celtics, who rolled through the Eastern Division with a 49–23 record, led by Bill Russell and his league-leading 22.7-rebound average.

This team was loaded with six future NBA Hall of Famers, including Russell, Bob Cousy, Sam Jones, Tommy Heinsohn, Bill Sharman, and Frank Ramsey. Most NBA experts picked the Celtics to easily win the title.

Compare this to Walton's team, the top-ranked and unbeaten UCLA Bruins. They were the Celtics of college basketball. Walton's team was considered one of the greatest college basketball teams of all time, with back-to-back 30–0 seasons that helped make up UCLA's 88-game winning streak. The Bruins went into the championship game as an overwhelming favorite, and won the school's seventh consecutive title.

233

THE GAMES:

The Hawks got a huge break in this series when Russell suffered an ankle injury in the third game of the finals.

In Walton's Final Four, Memphis State was at full strength, but it really didn't matter, since the Bruins rolled to an easy 21-point victory. Walton was unstoppable. What he accomplished was without question the greatest single performance by a collegian within the St. Louis city limits.

Things were not so easy for the Hawks, who returned to Kiel Auditorium with home-court advantage for Game 6. Even with that and an injured Russell playing at less than 100 percent, the Hawks and Celtics engaged in a classic confrontation that went down to the wire, with St. Louis winning 110–109 to capture the Hawks' first and only NBA title. They couldn't and wouldn't have done it without Pettit, who was spectacular from start to finish. He scored 31 points in the first three quarters, then put on a Hall-of-Fame fourth quarter, scoring 19 of St. Louis' last 21 points. His last two points, on a tip-in with 15 seconds remaining, put the Hawks ahead 110–107.

So who gets the edge? We're going with Pettit's 50-point game for several reasons. Pettit's game was done at basketball's highest level, the NBA finals. It was even more impressive because he did it against the Celtics, the NBA's greatest dynasty of all time. The Hawks' championship victory was the only time during Boston's stretch of 10 consecutive trips to the NBA finals that the Celtics did not win the championship. And even with a less-than-100-percent Bill Russell on the floor, Pettit still did it against a team loaded with future Hall of Famers.

If you add all those factors together, Pettit's game has to be considered the greatest individual basketball performance in St. Louis history.

COLLEGE EDITION

WHAT WAS THE SINGLE WORST MOMENT IN ST. LOUIS COLLEGE SPORTS HISTORY?

93 In the University of Missouri record book, it is known as "a game to remember; a game to forget."

In the hearts and guts of most Mizzou fans, it's known as "The #@*!!!, freakin' fifth down!"

Faurot Field was the site of one of college football's most historic—and disastrous—games. The date was October 6, 1990, when the eventual national champion Colorado Buffaloes pulled out a 33–31 victory over the Tigers, scoring the winning touchdown on what turned out to be a fifth down on the last play of the game.

The Tigers were on the verge of a monumental upset, leading 31–27, when Colorado embarked on a frantic march down the field in the final minute of play. With 31 seconds left, the Buffaloes picked up a first down to the Mizzou 3-yard line. On first down, CU quarterback Charles Johnson spiked the ball to stop the clock. On second down, tailback Eric Bieniemy ran up the middle to the 1-yard line and Colorado called its final time-out.

There were 18 seconds remaining, and that's when everything went wrong.

For some strange reason, no game official bothered to check with the sideline chain crew to see if they were flipping the down marker properly from second to third down.

Amazingly, on its home turf, Mizzou's own chain crew failed to change the down marker. When play resumed, Bieniemy was stopped for no gain at the line of scrimmage, and the clock ticked down to eight seconds before game officials stopped the clock briefly to clear up the scrum.

Still no one noticed that the down marker was wrong, so on what should have been fourth down, Johnson spiked the ball again and the game should have been over.

Now the clock was frozen at two seconds, and the marker said it was fourth down, when it was actually *fifth down.*

On the extra fourth down, the Colorado quarterback took the snap, then found a sliver of a hole behind right tackle Mark VanderPoel. Hit at the goal line, Johnson rolled over and extended the ball into the end zone and the officials signaled touchdown.

Only then did people begin to realize that something very bad (for Mizzou) had just happened, but by that time it was too late. Time had expired, giving the Tigers no chance to appeal the injustice. So instead of a memorable upset that would have spoiled Colorado's national championship season, the game went into the history books for a more dubious reason.

238

WHO WAS THE GREATEST MIZZOU BASKETBALL PLAYER OF ALL TIME?

This one is sure to register a ton of debate because there are so many worthy candidates to choose from. Do you go real old school with legends like Bill Stauffer or Norm Stewart? I just can't bring myself to consider either of these 1950s stars because the level of competition in college basketball back then was not anywhere near what it became in the 1970s and beyond.

So why not Willie Smith, the best pure scorer in school history? The guard from Las Vegas (1975–76) averaged 23.9 points during his two-year career. He was named an All-American in 1976, first-team All-Big Eight in 1975 and 1976, and the Big Eight Player of the Year in 1976. In 1976, he led Mizzou to its first conference title in 36 years (averaging a school-record 25.3 points a game), and the Tigers finished the season by reaching the Elite Eight in the 1976 NCAA Tournament. He was inducted into the Missouri Athletics Hall of Fame in 1991 and had his jersey number (#30) retired.

What keeps Smith from ultimate consideration is his brief career in Columbia. He was a brilliant comet who shot across the sky for only two seasons, which just isn't enough time to merit "all-time greatest"—certainly not when there are two other celebrated Mizzou stars who earned their keep for four seasons: Steve Stipanovich and Doug Smith.

Smith (1988–91) is likely the most talented individual player to ever suit up for the Tigers. The 6-foot-9 forward from Detroit is the only player in school history to reach 2,000 career points and 1,000 career rebounds during his four-year career. He ranks No. 2 on MU's career scoring list, with 2,184 points (17.1 ppg), and he capped off his senior year by averaging 23.6 points, gaining All-America honors, and earning back-to-back Big Eight Conference Player of the Year awards.

In every major statistical category, Steve Stipanovich (1980–83) ranks behind Smith, which doesn't exactly leave him as some end-of-the-bench third-stringer. The 6-foot-11 St. Louis native left Missouri as the school's career leader in scoring, rebounding, and blocked shots. Today, he still ranks fourth on the career scoring list, third in rebounding, and second in blocked shots. In his senior year in 1983, "Stepo" was a consensus All-American, the Big Eight Conference Player of the Year, and the second overall pick in the NBA draft while leading the Tigers to a 26–8 record.

Stipanovich's edge in this "all-time greatest" debate comes down to one category that is unmatched: He led Mizzou to four straight Big Eight regular-season titles. Winning championships ought to mean something, and in this debate, it does.

WHO WAS THE GREATEST MIZZOU FOOTBALL PLAYER OF ALL TIME?

95 In the history of Missouri football, 26 Tigers have gone on to earn first-team All-America honors. Three of the greatest and most legendary Mizzou All-Americans were tailback Johnny Roland and two future NFL Hall of Famers, tight end Kellen Winslow and cornerback Roger Wehrli.

Yet anyone with a keen sense of Mizzou football history would probably agree that the greatest of them all never earned first-team All-America honors (he was honorable mention). Brad Smith was not only the best football player to ever wear a Tigers uniform, he was by far the most exciting player to ever step on Faurot Field.

In typical Brad Smith fashion, his last game in a MU uniform typified the sort of performances Mizzou fans came to expect from him. The senior quarterback led Mizzou to a thrilling 2005 Independence Bowl victory over South Carolina, 38–31, after trailing by 21–0 in the first quarter.

Smith had 432 yards of total offense, including 282 yards passing (1 touchdown) and 150 yards rushing (3 touchdowns), and he completed 21 of 37 passes. The highlight of the show was a game-winning 59-yard run that was, typically, all improvisation. It was a broken play that he turned into an electrifying scamper with the entire Gamecock defense in pursuit.

Let's first deal with the lengthy records he owns, including a staggering 69 different MU, Big 12, and NCAA single-game, season, and career marks:

- He holds the NCAA Div. I-A career rushing record for quarterbacks, with 4,289 yards, and became the first NCAA Div. I-A quarterback to throw for 8,000 yards and rush for 4,000 yards in a career.
- He ended his career ranked fourth on the all-time NCAA career total offense chart, with 13,088 yards, almost double what the previous MU career record was (6,640 by Jeff Handy from 1991–94).
- With 2,304 passing yards and 1,301 rushing yards in 2005, he became the first player in NCAA Div. I-A history to achieve the 2,000/1,000 mark twice in his career (he also did it as a redshirt freshman in 2002).
- He is one of only three players in Div. I-A history to have four seasons of 2,500 yards of total offense, and is one of only six players to have three seasons of 3,000 yards of total offense.

For me, though, the defining memory of Brad Smith was watching him dismantle Nebraska in a 41–24 rout during his senior year in 2005. As fans and players at Faurot Field went positively crazy celebrating the victory, the hero of the day—the calm and collected Brad Smith—quietly shifted through the crowd and glided into the locker room. Everyone else in this joyful stadium wanted to celebrate one of the most amazing individual offensive shows in college football history.

Everyone, of course, but the calm, cool, and very collected Mr. Smith.

"Nah, I didn't want to get into that stuff," Smith said, shrugging his shoulders and flashing a slight smile. "I just tried to get in here as quick as I could. I just wanted to sit down somewhere."

Typically, he was the coolest man in the room. He had just put on one of the finest all-around offensive shows in college football history (246 yards rushing and 3 touchdowns; 234 yards passing for another touchdown) and he barely raised his pulse. It was just like he had done on the field, when he took off on a 45-yard score that gave the Tigers a 31–24 lead in the third quarter. It was a typical Smith dash; it seemed like he was floating in slow motion, yet a string of lunging Nebraska defenders dived into nothing but thin air.

Mizzou defensive tackle Lorenzo Williams raised his eyebrow on that one. "Ah, that's all smoke and mirrors," Williams said. "That's the Brad Smith illusion. Trust me; that boy's fast."

ST. LOUIS' GREATEST COLLEGE FOOTBALL TEAM:

The 1960 MU Tigers or the 1963 Illini?

96 Usually these "greatest team" arguments are complicated by attempting to compare apples to oranges. How do you sort through the best of the best when too often you're required to do it by evaluating teams from vastly different eras?

Luckily for us, we can avoid that nearly impossible mission with this conversation. The two most accomplished college football teams in modern St. Louis sports history (we will not bother to include the turn-of-the-century St. Louis University team that invented the forward pass; that was an entirely different game back then) actually competed in the same era. The 1960 Missouri team that "technically" finished with an unbeaten 11–0 mark and an Orange Bowl victory is a strong candidate for "best ever." So is the 1963 Big Ten championship Illinois team led by some guy named Dick Butkus.

Before we go any further, there's a very good reason why we're debating about the Illini in a St. Louis sports argument. With the city sitting just on the east side of the

Mississippi River and resting along the Missouri-Illinois border, Illinois sports teams—particularly the Illini and the Southern Illinois Salukis—are among a large collection of colleges that are considered "local" teams. If you pick up a St. Louis newspaper or turn on a local sportscast, you will see how much both Illinois and SIU are seriously covered and cared about.

So that's why the 1963 Illini deserve to be in the mix in this conversation. Looking back, that season was remarkable for any number of reasons. Begin with the surprising one-year turnaround from the 1962 season when Illinois lost its first five games and struggled to a 2–7 season and an eighth-place finish in the Big Ten conference. Yet only a few months later, the Illini became a national championship contender.

This team was led by sophomore fullback Jim Grabowski and quarterback Mike Taliaferro on offense, and Don Hansen and junior All-American Dick Butkus at linebacker. They beat future NFL star Craig Morton and Cal in the opener 10–0, then tied highly favored Ohio State 20–20, which let them and the rest of the country know that the Illini were for real. They would only lose one game the rest of the season, finishing 7–1–1, with only a midseason loss to Michigan blemishing the record. Moving from winless to the Rose Bowl in one year is pretty impressive.

Yet as impressive as Illinois' season was, Missouri's 1960 Tigers were a superior team, and here are just a few reasons why:

- It's hard to dispute that the 1963 Illini were a fluke. After that surprise turnaround, Illinois would have only three winning seasons over the next 11. It would take 18 more years for Illinois football to win more than six games in a season.

- When you look at the 1960 Mizzou Tigers, they not only had an impressive season in 1960, but it proved to merely be the start of something big. The 1960 team started off the Dan Devine era of success in Columbia. In the 1960s, Devine's teams had a .762 winning percentage (77–22–6), the seventh best in the nation for the decade, and the Tigers never lost more than three games in a season.

- While Illinois would end the 1963 season ranked higher than the Tigers would finish the 1960 season (No. 3 to No. 5), the 1960 Tigers went from unranked in the preseason to the No. 1 team in America, and went into the final game of the regular season ranked at the top of both the AP and UPI with a 9–0 record.

What ultimately separated Missouri from Illinois was the opportunity to win a national championship. MU was within one game of winning a national championship in 1960. A victory over unranked archrival Kansas, plus a victory in a New Year's bowl game, would give the Tigers their first national championship.

So you know how this went, right?

KU crushed those championship dreams with a 23–7 victory. Later, after it was discovered that Kansas had used an ineligible player—businessman and KU alum Bud Adams, who would later become owner of the Houston Oilers and Tennessee Titans, was found guilty of giving players special privileges—Missouri was awarded a forfeit victory.

So technically, after their 21–14 Orange Bowl triumph over Navy, the Tigers finished 11–0.

The poll voters didn't see it that way, and instead of maintaining their No. 1 ranking, Mizzou fell to fifth. But in our poll of the best all-time St. Louis college football teams, the 1960 Tigers finished No. 1.

ST. LOUIS' GREATEST COLLEGE BASKETBALL TEAM:

The 1948 Billikens, the 2005 Illini, or the 1989 Flyin' Illini?

97 When it comes down to it, trying to sort out the best college basketball teams in St. Louis sports history involves a little expansive geography. With only one Division I team inside the city limits, we have to consider the state schools in the general two-hour vicinity.

Missouri just doesn't meet the grade because none of the Tigers' 21 NCAA tournament teams have ever made it beyond the Elite Eight. Missouri State has no great post-season journeys, either. Southern Illinois has grown into a consistent national power, but the best the Salukis can present are two Sweet 16 trips.

That leaves us with St. Louis U's 1948 NCAA champi-onship team and lllinois' two Final Four squads—the 1989 Flyin' Illini and the 2005 national runner-ups.

Let's try and separate the Illinois teams first. The 2005 Illinois team had the greatest season in school history, finishing with a 37–2 record, narrowly losing to a powerful

North Carolina squad in the NCAA championship game in St. Louis. That 37–2 record tied the winningest season in the history of college basketball. The Illini were ranked No. 1 in the nation for 15 consecutive weeks and won 32 straight games in that season.

They had five players average in double figures in scoring (Luther Head at 15.9, Dee Brown at 13.3, Deron Williams at 12.5, Roger Powell at 12.0, and James Augustine at 10.1). Bruce Weber was named college coach of the year by 10 separate organizations and Brown, Williams, and Head were named All-Americans. They rolled through the Big Ten with a 15–1 record and back-to-back conference titles, adding the Big Ten tournament title to their already impressive list of accomplishments.

After that showy résumé, I'm not even sure why we're having a conversation about any other Illinois team. As good and exciting as the 1989 Illini were, they simply don't come up to the same level as the 2005 Illini. The 1989 squad was 31–5, but finished second in the Big Ten regular season (there was no Big Ten tournament until 1998). The 1989 team reached the Final Four, but lost in the national semifinals to Michigan. The Flyin' Illini had a lot of exciting players, but lacked the depth of the 2005 team.

So our team for consideration that resides east of the Mississippi River is unquestionably the 2005 Illinois team that barely lost the championship game at the Edward Jones Dome.

The only team on the western shore of the Mississippi is St. Louis U's 1947–48 team that won the National Invitation Tournament championship, which at the time was the equivalent of the national collegiate title. So is it possible to pick a team that finished as a national runner-up over a team that won the entire national championship?

I actually think it's a no-brainer. Yes, the Billikens were national champs, but back then, it only took three playoff games to win the title. SLU's record was only 24–3 and they finished second in the Missouri Valley Conference regular season (no postseason tournament). But finally, can we get real? Come on, it was 1948. The game was slower back then and played mostly below the rim. Do you honestly think those scrappy, gritty, gutsy 1948 Billikens could have hung athletically with the 2005 Illini, even with All-America forward "Easy Ed" Macauley?

The answer is a definitive "no."

So the greatest team hands down is the 2005 Illinois national championship runner-ups.

Put this one under a large headline that reads, "It seemed like a good idea at the time."

Four years ago, some very smart decision-makers at St. Louis University had an inspiration. For the fifth time since 1982, it was time to once again go conference shopping to find a place for their basketball team to play. Conference USA's showpiece team Louisville was being gobbled up by the basketball powerhouse Big East Conference in a move that also strengthened the Big East's status among the BCS football power structure.

So Doug Willard, SLU's athletics director at the time, had a hunch. Like so many other BCS conferences, the Big East, he figured, was going to have another major split in the future, shedding its non-football schools and becoming an even larger football-first conference. And when that inevitable split came and Georgetown, Villanova, DePaul, St. John's, and Seton Hall were kicked out of the Big East, an enormous super-Jesuit schools basketball conference would be created that might spread from New York in the

East to Gonzaga in the West. And when that conference was formed, St. Louis U had to find a way to become a part of that incredible basketball conference.

The Billikens needed to elevate their college hoops profile, and the best way to do that seemed to be by joining an East Coast-dominated conference like the Atlantic 10. Staying in Conference USA was not the most attractive option, and neither was moving to the mid-major Missouri Valley Conference.

Oops.

Four years later, the Billikens and all of their alumni base are experiencing that gut-gurgling sensation known affectionately as buyer's remorse.

This will be SLU's third year in the Atlantic 10, and when the Billikens go to the conference tournament next March, they will have to travel nearly 900 miles across six states to Atlantic City, New Jersey, to play a tournament game in a half-empty arena with only a handful of SLU fans in attendance. There will be no local television to speak of, and no local or national buzz surrounding the tourney. Officially, no one in the SLU athletic community is saying this is a bad thing.

Then again, they don't have to, because anyone can see that it's a bad thing.

"When I first heard that theory for why they were going to the A-10, I have to say the first thing that came to my mind was, 'Wow, that might be the dumbest thing I've ever heard,'" a prominent conference commissioner told me during last year's Final Four. "If they're waiting on the Big East to split up again, they could be in for a very long wait, because I don't see that sort of thing happening any time soon."

The official stance of the school is that selecting the Atlantic 10 was an overall marketing strategy in SLU President Rev. Lawrence Biondi's big picture to raise the national profile of St. Louis University and attract a more diverse student body. But basketball people still are scratching their heads because the landscape of college basketball didn't exactly change the way SLU envisioned it.

The Billikens should have chosen the Missouri Valley Conference, and now it is painfully obvious that going to the Atlantic 10 was a bad move. Why? Last season more than 65,000 fans crammed into the Scottrade Center—St. Louis U's home court—for the Missouri Valley Conference Tournament. Arch Madness was in full effect, with the semifinals and finals watched by record crowds (22,612 both nights) and a nationally televised audience on CBS.

The MVC is now considered one of the top five or six basketball conferences in the country, while the Atlantic 10 is sliding deeper into mediocrity. SLU could have been—should have been—in the MVC. And now four years after choosing the Atlantic 10 over the Missouri Valley, there is a quiet rumbling among local alumni who are having major second thoughts. In 2003, the MVC was just your generic mid-major conference. Now it's the chic, ultra-hip college conference everybody loves.

253

It's time for SLU to make a U-turn. It's time to admit that buyer's remorse. It's not so much that picking the A-10 was a bad idea; it's just that, in hindsight, not picking the MVC seems like such a gargantuan gaffe.

Four years ago, I firmly believed SLU was making the right move. Today, I realize how wrong I was. The college basketball landscape has changed since 2003. The predicted split of the Big East Conference into a super-football conference hasn't happened and probably never will. Nor has the creation of the super-Jesuit schools basketball conference that was supposed to crop up out of the rubble of the second Big East split.

Instead came the totally unforeseen meteoric rise of the MVC. It's time for St. Louis U to review geography. Why cross six states and 900 miles to hardly make a ripple, when you can literally walk a mile down the street and be a part of a bigger, better deal going on in your own building?

WHO WILL REACH THE FINAL FOUR FIRST:

SLU or Southern Illinois?

99 When I first began writing this book in the late winter of 2006, it never even crossed my mind that it would be an interesting idea to compare St. Louis University's mediocre basketball program with that of the richly successful mid-major powerhouse in Carbondale, Illinois, known as Southern Illinois.

Through three generations of head coaches over the last decade, the Salukis of SIU have risen from mid-major obscurity and transformed themselves into a legitimate and consistent Top 25 program in America.

St. Louis U could not even join the conversation.

With only three trips to the NCAA tournament over the last 13 years and none over the last seven seasons, no one took the Billikens seriously on the St. Louis basketball landscape. If you ranked SLU's place on the local hoop food chain, it would have fallen far behind Mizzou, Illinois, Southern Illinois, and maybe even Missouri State in terms of generating local fan excitement.

But all of that changed in April of 2007 when the university fired Brad Soderberg and replaced him with Rick Majerus.

SLU is relevant again. Majerus, one of the most successful coaches in college basketball (over 400 coaching victories, consistent runs to the NCAA tournament, proven record of producing NBA draft picks), forces everyone to take the Billikens seriously now.

I firmly believe if his health can hold up, Majerus can turn SLU into a major player on the college hoop landscape. He will out-recruit Mizzou, Illinois, and even SIU on more than one or two occasions when the schools battle for kids in the deep local prep talent pool. That would have been unheard of a few months before Majerus arrived. But kids know Majerus can coach. They know what his basketball résumé says. That will definitely entice plenty of them to stay home and enjoy the benefits of an urban college campus and a spanking new arena.

But the bigger player—and most consistent one—in my mind remains Southern Illinois, particularly with Chris Lowery working the sidelines.

Southern Illinois sent a very clear message to everyone in the basketball community that they are ready to play on the same level with the likes of Mizzou and Illinois (and now with SLU, too) after the end of the 2006–07 season. The message was sent via a thick check book, when athletics director Mario Moccia rounded up enough alumni support to re-sign his 34-year-old coach to a hefty new contract reportedly worth over $750,000 a year. It was a definitive message to anyone who was watching that Southern

Illinois would prevent the big-money universities with deep pockets from snatching away their coaching prodigy.

So now things have gotten quite interesting on the local basketball scene.

It was always a given that Mizzou and Illinois had the economic wherewithal and university and alumni commitment to help their programs try to reach the Final Four. But until recently, it seemed farfetched to believe SIU or SLU could harbor such lofty hoop dreams.

Not any more.

The Salukis' fantastic run to the Sweet 16 in 2007—and missing out on an Elite Eight trip by a whisker in a tight loss to Kansas—proved that Lowery knows how to keep Southern Illinois on that consistent Top 10 to Top 35 level for as long as he's in Carbondale. He has also given everyone a legitimate belief that something bigger is possible.

For a program that comes from a traditional mid-major conference like the Missouri Valley Conference, what the Salukis have done—beginning with Bruce Weber, and now rising even higher under Lowery—has put their program on the verge of giddy Gonzaga-like levels.

"I think the Gonzaga comparison is a good one," Ohio State director of athletics Gene Smith told me. "With the success they've had over the past few years, it's easy to see that they're fully capable of rising to that level and become sort of the Gonzaga of the Midwest. And I also think it's reasonable to assume that they can remain on that

257

level for a long time, maybe even staying on even footing with Illinois every year because of the talent pool of high school talent in Illinois and the St. Louis area. But one huge key to keeping it going seems to be taking care of Chris. He's a rising star in the coaching ranks."

These are great times for Southern Illinois. They are also critical times, as well. While this great stretch of regular- and postseason success has, as Lowery says, flooded the basketball mainstream "with our brand name," the next step in the evolutionary process to transcend mid-major labeling is to duplicate Gonzaga's NCAA tournament success (nine consecutive trips to the tournament, including an Elite Eight trip).

Becoming the "new" Gonzaga won't be easy, but the surest way to make it happen was retaining Lowery's services for a few more years. The relentless work ethic he preaches to his players is the same high standard he expects of himself. No one outworks Lowery when it comes to basketball, whether it's on the court or the recruiting trail. In only three years in Carbondale, he has turned into arguably the best basketball pitchman in the St. Louis area. Lowery and his staff have consistently come into St. Louis and culled unrefined gems out of the local high schools that everyone else overlooked or ignored. And now with the program rising to a Top 15 nationally ranked level, Lowery has stepped up his recruiting game even more, already beating everyone to two of the best juniors in St. Louis—McCluer North's Anthony Booker and Torres Roundtree.

But Majerus has crowded his way into Lowery's territory. His national status puts him in a perfect position to intrude on the most significant local recruiting class in recent memory in St. Louis. Over the next couple years, there will be several tall and very talented young men on the open market looking for a place to play college ball. It will be a furious race among Mizzou, SLU, Southern Illinois, and Illinois to keep them local.

I think both SLU and Southern Illinois now have the potential to end up in the Final Four. Whoever manages to harvest the most high school stars out of St. Louis will be the one that wins the race to the Final Four. If Majerus stays at SLU for at least five years, the Billikens have a decent shot to do it over the long haul, but because Lowery already has his established program in place, the Salukis—who have been close before—will get there first.

THE BIG FINISH

WHAT'S WRONG WITH SPORTS IN ST. LOUIS? (AND WHAT I'D DO TO FIX THEM)

100

I am your St. Louis sports czar, and I am in charge. If there's something wrong, I will not only tell you what it is, I will fix it, too.

I demand emotional reparations for Ozzie Smith. It is time to bring the Hall of Fame shortstop out of exile, bring him back into the Cardinals family, give him a prominent seat at the table, and force he and Tony La Russa to kiss and make up (even if we all know they won't mean it).

For just one off-season, I want Cardinals management to spend money like the teams do in Boston and New York. I want wild and lavish spending. I want them to have an unlimited budget and exceed it. Why? Because I just want to see one time how the other half lives.

I want all ill-informed, pandering gas bags to be taken off the local sports talk airwaves. Mean-spirited ranting is not entertainment, it's mean-spirited ranting.

And speaking of sports talk radio, I want the "Morning Grind" to be re-born, but I know it never will.

I would put Jim Hanifan in the Rams and football Cardinals ring of honor. He is the original football poet laureate of St. Louis, a charming, occasionally vulgar historian of the NFL in this town.

St. Louis should be on the NCAA's regular Final Four rotation. So as sports czar, I would snap my fingers and fast track the construction of the Bottle District urban renewal around the Edward Jones Dome. I would also remove all the red tape and political nonsense that is slowing down the construction of Busch Stadium's Ballpark Village, too. The NCAA loves to put on the Final Four in cities that have river walks and entertainment districts in convenient walking distance to everything.

Too many St. Louis citizens fail to understand that the fastest route to a downtown rebirth is to realize that it should model itself after Indianapolis and make sports its primary industry, college sports most of all. This town ought to be hosting NCAA basketball tournaments every other year, and competing for the Big Ten and Big 12 basketball tournaments and football conference championships, too.

I want to see a round-robin college basketball tournament in St. Louis every December involving Mizzou, Illinois, St. Louis University, and Southern Illinois. It should be in the Dome and it should draw 45,000 people every game.

I want to see Missouri and Illinois football become relevant nationally. With two teams in major conferences that are dominant football conferences, the Tigers and Illini should be legitimate contenders for a BCS bowl game every three or four years.

I want everyone in St. Louis to get over their denial of Mark McGwire. He cheated, okay?

I want Mark McGwire to do what he said he was going to do, which is be a champion of the anti-steroid movement in sports. And I want him to admit he did it, too.

And if he doesn't do this, I want them to take his name off the I-70 Interstate.

Actually, I want them to take his name off the highway signs no matter what.

I want grown-ups to get out of kids sports. Kids don't play pick-up games anymore. Everything is organized by adults and it's just not as much fun to play sports when some old man is screaming at you.

On a similar note, I want all suburban schools and play-grounds to remove those damned signs from their fences that say you can't use their fields, courts, or playgrounds without prior permission. Ball fields are not like doctor's offices, so you shouldn't need to make an appointment to play on them.

I also want to go to a high school game and enjoy it. I do not want to hear grown-ups sitting in the stands grumbling about why a gangly 6-foot-6 15-year-old can't hit a jump shot. I want to be able to go to a game and not hear somebody's father or uncle or third cousin twice removed yelling out instructions to a kid that conflict with the coach's instructions. Parents are not coaches. They are not scouts. They are not television commentators. They are parents. Sit down, shut up, and let your kids enjoy themselves.

I want St. Louis football fans to start appreciating how good Marc Bulger is.

And while we're at it, I want St. Louis sports fans to stop obsessing so much with past heroes that they fail to appreciate the new ones.

And oh yeah, Whitey Herzog's not coming back. Get over it.

Here's what I don't get. St. Louis sports fans are notorious for being parochial, for being reluctant to trust any outsider, particularly their favorite perceived villains—the all-encompassing "know-it-all East Coast–biased media"— yet they obsess over that same biased media ignoring them. So I will wave my hand and end this senseless obsession with the so-called East Coast–biased media. So what if they don't care about our teams? Since when do you need "outsiders" to validate you? When the Cardinals were in the World Series, everyone all over the country was writing about the Cards. When the Rams were in the Super Bowl, everyone was gushing over the Greatest Show on Turf. Here's what's really important: winning. Winning is the only validation St. Louis teams need.

I want St. Louis baseball fans to stop leaving games in the sixth inning. This ain't Los Angeles, people. There's not going to be an hour-long backup on I-40 after games at Busch Stadium.

I want all St. Louis sports fans to stop feeling like it's necessary every time they call a talk radio show that they give us their personal sports résumé before telling us what they think. It doesn't matter how many years you've been a personal seat license holder, or that you once knew Stan Musial's wife's, cousin's, neighbor's sister's hairdresser. I don't need to know that you could have played minor-league baseball or have been a loyal Cardinals fan since the "Gas House Gang" was in Sportsman's Park, okay? Please... *PUL-eeeeeez!!!!* Just cut to the chase and tell us what you think without the annoying two-minute preamble.

But most of all, I really want St. Louis sports fans to remember something. Every time you're watching a game on television, or listening to the radio, or even reading about a game, and feel so angry that you want to throw something, remember that sports are still games, and games are still supposed to be fun.

INDEX
by Subject

S

St. John's University, 251

St. Louis Blues
1981 season, 79–81
2000 season, 79–81
best players, 25–28
comeback, record-breaking
(2005), 64
Davidson, John, 228–29
fan frustration, 184–87
Keenan, Mike, 195–96
Monday Night Miracle, 65–66,
185
owners, 189–92
Plante, Jacques, 192–93
St. Louis Hawks and, 225
Shanahan, Brendan, 187–88
trades (best), 87–88
trades (worst), 94–96
Turgeon, Pierre, 193–94
Western Conference finals,
65–66, 185

St. Louis Browns, 6

St. Louis Cardinals (baseball)
announcers, 206–8
attendance, 204–5
best players, 7–18
Busch stadium, 18, 137,
198–200, 208–9, 211–13
Chicago Cubs rivalry, 100–102
corporate sponsorship, 227
Denkinger, Don, 115–22

dream team, 123–41
El Birdos, 68–73
fans, 201–5, 263, 264–65
Gas House Gang, 9, 68–73, 134,
135, 138
Gibson, Bob, 103–5
Herzog, Whitey, 264
La Russa versus Smith feud, 261
managers, best, 111–15
McGee, Willie, 109–10
McGwire, Mark, 106–8, 263
Molina, Yadier, 229
National League Championship
Series (1985), 14
National League Championship
Series (2005), 57–59
nicknames, 217–18
Robinson, Jackie, 54–57, 221
Shannon, Mike, 39
Swifties, 68–73, 114
trades (best), 84–86
trades, worst, 92–93
World Series (1926), 125–26
World Series (1931), 134
World Series (1934), 134
World Series (1942), 70
World Series (1946), 60–61, 70,
139
World Series (1964), 136
World Series (1967), 72
World Series (1982), 114,
127–28
World Series (1985), 115–22

271

THE BEST ST. LOUIS SPORTS ARGUMENTS

273

"fifth down" game, 237–38
relevance of, 262–63
University of Nebraska, 242–43
University of North Carolina, 249
University of Notre Dame, 53
University of South Carolina,
241–42

V

Villanova University, 251

W

Washington Capitols, 186
Washington Senators, 51
Washington University, 221–22
Whiteyball, 113
World Boxing Association (WBA),
37
World Cup (1950), 215
World Series
1926, 125–26
1931, 134
1934, 134
1942, 70
1946, 60–61, 70, 139
1964, 136
1967, 72
1982, 85, 127–28
1985, 115–22
2006, 113
World War II, 71

INDEX
by Name

THE BEST ST. LOUIS SPORTS ARGUMENTS

281

283

ACKNOWLEDGMENTS

Thanks to my editor at Sourcebooks, Shana Drehs, for her productive prodding, tireless editing, and creative instincts. Without her behind-the-scenes partnership, there is no way this project would have gotten off the ground or reached a successful completion.

ABOUT THE AUTHOR

St. Louis Post-Dispatch columnist Bryan Burwell arrived in St. Louis in 2002 with a distinguished national reputation. After only four years in the city, *St. Louis Magazine* hailed him as the best reporter in St. Louis on its 2006 "A List."

In his 30-plus-year career in sports journalism, Burwell has proven to be an accomplished multimedia star as an award-winning sports writer, columnist, and television and radio commentator. As a print journalist, Burwell established a national reputation writing for some of the most prestigious newspapers in America, including *USA Today*, the *Sporting News*, the *Detroit News*, *New York Newsday*, and the *New York Daily News*. In addition to his current position with the *St. Louis Post-Dispatch* and a national column on MSNBC.com, he has also contributed to *Hoop* magazine and *Sports Illustrated*. As an author, Burwell's first book, *At the Buzzer! Havlicek Steals, Erving Soars, Magic Deals, Michael Scores: The Greatest Moments in NBA History*, was published in October, 2001, and his writing has been published in several sports anthologies. He has won writing awards from the Associated Press Sports Editors, the National Association of Black Journalists, United Press International, the Professional Basketball Writers Association, and the Professional Football Writers Association of America. In 2004, Burwell was nominated for a local Emmy® for his sports commentary with Fox 2 (St. Louis).

On the television side, Burwell spent 14 years with HBO as a feature reporter on Inside the NFL's "Cover Story" segment. He was part of the program's groundbreaking 2002 Sports Emmy win for "Outstanding Studio Show— Weekly." He also spent four years with the Emmy-winning *Real Sports with Bryant Gumbel*. His other television credits include work as an NBA correspondent for Turner Broadcasting and CNN. He currently works as a contributor to the St. Louis news channel Fox 2. Burwell is a studio analyst for Fox 2's *Rams Gameday Live*, and does weekly sports commentary for Fox 2. Burwell is a regular panelist on ESPN's *Jim Rome Is Burning* and *The Sports Reporters*, and is a contributor to ESPN's *Sports Century* documentary series. He did voice-over work for the ESPN documentary on the late sports writing legend Ralph Wiley in 2005, and in February of 2007 hosted a nationally televised documentary on the Negro Baseball Leagues called *The Color of Change*.

Burwell, a former scholarship track and field athlete at Virginia State University, lives in Wildwood, Missouri, with his wife, Dawnn, and daughter, Victoria.